4/95

PRESENTING

Madeleine L'Engle

Twayne's United States Authors Series
Young Adult Authors

Patricia J. Campbell, General Editor

TUSAS 622

MADELEINE L'ENGLE
Photograph © James Phillips 1989

PRESENTING

Madeleine L'Engle

Donald R. Hettinga

Twayne Publishers • New York
Maxwell Macmillan Canada • Toronto
Maxwell Macmillan International • New York   Oxford   Singapore   Sydney

Twayne's United States Authors Series No. 622

Presenting Madeleine L'Engle
Donald R. Hettinga

Twayne Publishers`   Maxwell Macmillan Canada, Inc.
Macmillan Publishing Company   1200 Eglinton Avenue East
866 Third Avenue   Suite 200
New York, New York 10022   Don Mills, Ontario M3C 3N1

Library of Congress Cataloging-in-Publication Data

Hettinga, Donald R., 1953–
    Presenting Madeleine L'Engle / Donald R. Hettinga.
      p.   cm. — (Twayne's United States authors series ; TUSAS
622. Young adult authors)
    Includes bibliographical references.
    ISBN 0-8057-8222-2
    1. L'Engle, Madeleine—Criticism and interpretation.   2. Young
adult fiction, American—History and criticism.   I. Series:
Twayne's United States authors series ; 622.   II. Series: Twayne's
United States authors series.   Young adult authors.
PS3523.E55Z68   1993
813'.54—dc20   93-9188
                                           CIP

10 9 8 7 6 5 4 3 2 1 (hc)
10 9 8 7 6 5 4 3 2 1 (pb)

Printed in the United States of America

For Kim

Contents

Foreword

The advent of Twayne's Young Adult Author Series in 1985 was a response to the growing stature and value of adolescent literature and the lack of serious critical evaluation of the new genre. The first volume in the series was heralded as marking the coming-of-age of young adult fiction.

The aim of the series is twofold. First, it enables young readers to research the work of their favorite authors, and to see them as real people. Each volume is written in a lively, readable style and attempts to present in an attractive, accessible format a vivid portrait of the author as a person.

Second, the series provides teachers and librarians with insights and background material for promoting and teaching young adult novels. Each of the biocritical studies is a serious literary analysis of one author's work (or one sub-genre within young adult literature), with attention to plot structure, theme, character, setting, and imagery. In addition, many of the series writers delve deeper into the creative writing process by tracking down early drafts or unpublished manuscripts by their subject authors, consulting with their editors or other mentors, and examining influences from literature, film, or social movements.

Many of the contributing authors of the series are among the leading scholars and critics of adolescent literature. Some are even young adult novelists themselves. Most of the studies are based on extensive interviews with the subject author, and each includes an exhaustive study of his or her work. Although the general format is the same, the individual volumes are uniquely shaped by their subjects, and each brings a different perspective to the classroom.

The goal of the series is to produce a succinct but comprehensive study of the life and art of every leading young adult author writing in the United States today. The books trace how that art has been accepted by readers and critics, evaluate its place in the developing field of adolescent literature, and—perhaps most important—inspire a reading and re-reading of this quality fiction that speaks so directly to young people about their life's experiences.

PATRICIA J. CAMPBELL, General Editor

Preface

In a recent collection of essays, novelist Frederick Buechner expresses frustration with the usual etymology of *adolescence,* which defines the term as deriving from "the Latin verb *adolescere,* made up of *ad,* meaning toward, and *alescere,* meaning to grow." Buechner's complaint is that this etymology makes the process sound "too tidy," that it suggests that being a young adult is simply a matter of size and time and that as soon as a person passes a certain chronological or physiological point, he or she is no longer adolescent, no longer a young adult.

Though he was sixty-four at the time that he wrote this particular essay and though his "acne cleared up around 1945," he explains that his acne and his adolescence are still very much a part of his inner world. Consequently, he suggests an alternative etymology for *adolescence*, an etymology of his own manufacture, but one that I think Madeleine L'Engle would find convincing. Buechner proposes that the term might well be "made up of the Latin preposition *ad,* meaning toward, and the Latin noun *dolor,* meaning pain." Adolescents, in this definition, are "those who are in the process of discovering pain itself, of trying somehow to come to terms with pain" creatively in a manner that makes life more than simple survival. In explaining what he means by this focus on pain, he notes how young children can quite often seem to face the brokenness of their worlds—the alcoholic parents, the adults that abuse them or at least let them down—with amazing resilience, up to a point. "A bad day comes," he observes. "Then maybe a day that is not so bad or even a good day. Then maybe a bad one again. But by and large children do not seem to keep score. Adolescence, as I etymologize the term, starts when score-keeping starts."[1]

I think Madeleine L'Engle would appreciate Buechner's ficti-tious etymology for at least two reasons. The first is that on one level that is what many of her books for young adults are about—scorekeeping, or, at least, questioning the pain. Meg Murry won-ders why she and her brother just don't fit in anywhere. Vicky Austin wonders why people she loves have to die and ponders why her family fails to understand her. Sandy and Dennys Murry won-der how God could let a young woman die, a young woman whom they love very much. Polly O'Keefe wonders how a woman who claims to love her could also try to molest her. The second reason is that just as this etymology suggests that adolescence isn't merely for adolescents, it also suggests something L'Engle has been claiming as long as she has been writing, that young adult literature isn't just for young adults. Stories are stories, she as-serts, and stories are for everyone.

But L'Engle's novels are about much more than scorekeeping. They are about living creatively, about living morally. If they are sometimes about pain, they are also many times about joy. They are about life. Like life, good fiction is complex, and while I at-tempt to address the principal themes of the novels in this analy-sis of L'Engle's fiction for young adults, I know that I haven't addressed all the themes. There is much more that can be said about all of the works I discuss here, and I hope that this book stimulates such discussion.

Acknowledgments

I have to begin by thanking my wife, Kimberly Gilmore Hettinga, for her ideas and support throughout this project. For what she has given, there really is no adequate means of expressing gratitude, but this is my attempt to try.

I am also grateful to Calvin College for the sabbatical leave of absence that it granted me to work on this study and to the Calvin College Alumni Association for its generous financial support. I am also indebted to the Midwest Faculty Seminar and The University of Chicago for its fellowship support and for the use of The University of Chicago libraries.

My research was also greatly aided by two of the libraries that hold Madeleine L'Engle's papers, and I wish to express my gratitude to the de Grummond Children's Literature Research Collection in the McCain Library and Archives of the University of Southern Mississippi and to the Madeleine L'Engle Collection of the Buswell Memorial Library Archives and Special Collections of Wheaton College.

I am thankful, too, for the hard work of two very diligent research assistants, Lisa Joy Limburg and Lisa Spoelhof.

Finally, I must express my indebtedness to the editor of this series, Patricia J. Campbell, whose judicious suggestions and sharp editorial pencil made this a stronger book.

Chronology

1918 Born Madeleine L'Engle Camp, November 29, in New York, N.Y.

1929 Moves to a château in the French Alps

1930 Is sent to a boarding school in Switzerland

1932 Returns to United States; lives in northern Florida

1933 Is sent to Ashley Hall boarding school in Charleston, South Carolina

1935 Father dies of pneumonia

1936 L'Engle enrolls in Smith College.

1941 Graduates from Smith.

1941 Moves to apartment in New York, N.Y.

1943 Understudies role in *Uncle Harry* on Broadway.

1945 Receives role in *The Cherry Orchard;* meets Hugh Franklin.

1945 *The Small Rain.*

1946 Marries Hugh Franklin.

1946 *Ilsa.*

1946 L'Engle and Franklin purchase Crosswicks.

1947 Josephine born.

1949 *And Both Were Young;* revised 1983.

1951 *Camilla Dickinson;* revised 1965.

1952   Bion born.

1952   L'Engle and Franklin purchase and run general store.

1957   Maria comes to live with the family.

1957   *A Winter's Love.*

1958   L'Engle and Franklin sell general store; take cross-country camping trip.

1960   *Meet the Austins*

1962   *A Wrinkle in Time*

1963   John Newbery Medal for *A Wrinkle in Time.*

1963   *The Moon by Night*

1964   *The Twenty-four Days Before Christmas: An Austin Family Story*

1965   *The Arm of the Starfish*

1966   *The Love Letters*

1967   *The Journey with Jonah.*

1968   *The Young Unicorns.*

1968   The first section of *The Small Rain* republished as *Prelude.*

1969   Austrian State Literary Prize for *The Moon by Night.*

1969   *Dance in the Desert.*

1969   *Lines Scribbled on an Envelope, and Other Poems.*

1970   *Intergalactic P.S. 3.*

1971   *The Other Side of the Sun.*

1972   *A Circle of Quiet.*

1973   *A Wind in the Door.*

1974   *Summer of the Great-Grandmother.*

1974   *Prayers for Sunday.*

1974 *Everyday Prayers.*

1976 *Dragons in the Waters*

1977 *The Irrational Season.*

1978 *A Swiftly Tilting Planet.*

1978 University of Southern Mississippi Medal.

1978 *The Weather of the Heart.*

1979 *Ladder of Angels: Scenes from the Bible Illustrated by the Children of the World.*

1980 American Book Award for *A Swiftly Tilting Planet.*

1980 *A Ring of Endless Light.*

1981 *The Anti-Muffins.*

1981 Newbery Honor Award for *A Ring of Endless Light.*

1982 *The Sphinx at Dawn: Two Stories.*

1983 *Walking on Water: Reflections on Faith and Art.*

1984 Sophie award.

1984 *A House like a Lotus.*

1984 *And It Was Good: Reflections on Beginnings.*

1984 *Dare to Be Creative.*

1985 Regina Medal.

1986 *Many Waters.*

1986 *A Stone for a Pillow: Journeys with Jacob.*

1986 Hugh Franklin dies.

1988 *Two-Part Invention.*

1989 *Sold into Egypt: Joseph's Journey into Human Being.*

1989 *An Acceptable Time.*

1990 *The Glorious Impossible.*

1992 *Certain Women.*

1. Living By Story

We turn to stories and pictures and music because they show us
who and what and why we are, and what our relationship is to
life and death.

—*A Circle of Quiet*

You need not listen long to Madeleine L'Engle to hear her talk
about the importance of story. Her vocation is that of storyteller
and story itself is part of her story. "Story," she writes, "helped me
learn to live."[1] Already as a girl of five or six, she was ordering her
life by the stories she heard and wrote. Troubled by the horrific
images coming from the trenches of World War I, including that of
her father who, though he would live until Madeleine was eighteen, was weakened by mustard gas, she "tried to heal her fear
with stories, stories which gave . . . courage, stories which af-
firmed that ultimately love is stronger than hate" (*Walking,* 53).
The theme would be one that would inform her life's work, for her
fiction and nonfiction alike suggest that for her story was far from
the popular notion of escape and entertainment, but was instead
a mode of living "creatively" rather than "fearfully" (*Walking,* 53).
Her fiction, while not rigidly autobiographical as, for example,
Ernest Hemingway's, is yet informed and sometimes shaped by
the experiences of her life.

1

On 29 November 1918, just after the armistice that ended World War I, Madeleine L'Engle Camp was born in New York City to Charles Wadworth Camp and Madeleine Barnett Camp. Her early life with her parents left her much time to pass with stories. She ate meals by herself and spent much time away from her parents, who were both active in the New York arts scene—her mother an accomplished pianist and her father a drama and music critic for the *Herald-Evening Sun*. Her parents had been married for almost two decades before she was born, and so, as L'Engle recounts it, though she "was a very much wanted baby, the pattern of their lives was already well established and a child was not part of that pattern."[2] That life-style, however, meant lots of parties, and L'Engle recalls sneaking from her room and hiding under the piano listening to opera singers or to her mother playing for guests. Some of the images both of that solitude and of that New York life make their way into L'Engle's fourth novel, *Camilla*.[3]

The solitude made for a lot of time for reading for the young Madeleine, and many of the books she encountered as a child greatly influenced her life and her writing. One of her favorites at nine or ten years of age was L. M. Montgomery's *Emily of New Moon*. Emily, the central character of that novel, became L'Engle's heroine. Both L'Engle and Emily "were ecstatic over the beauties of this planet." Both wanted to be writers. Both had a bit of "what the Scots called 'Second Sight.'" Both had fathers who were ill. L'Engle explains that just as "Emily's father was dying from diseased lungs," her own "father was dying from lungs which had been mustard gassed in that war that was supposed to end war, but which started a century of war." But perhaps most significant, L'Engle reports that Emily helped her keep her own "Madeleineness," allowing her "to retain a sense of validity" in the face of peers and teachers who did not understand her.[4]

Other books offered other models. E. Nesbit's Bastable children gave her ordinary children to identify with, and Frances Hodgson Burnett's Mary Lennox (in *The Secret Garden*) provided the example of a heroine who, though she is "nasty and self-centered and spoiled," still "has a strong sense of survival," something that

L'Engle needed in her school situations. From Mary she also learned the important lesson "that a person who has heroic qualities is *human*, and does not have to be perfect" (L'Engle, "Heroic," 121–22), a lesson that L'Engle passes on to Vicky Austin, Meg Murry, and several other heroines that she creates. Some books offered heroes that were simply fun. One such character was Dennys the Dragon; L'Engle so enjoyed the way that he heats up the bedsheets and loyally performs other domestic tasks around his castle that she named Dennys, one of the Murry twins, after him (L'Engle, "Heroic," 124).

Yet the writer who had the most profound influence on L'Engle as a child was George MacDonald. Both MacDonald and his characters loomed large in her life. In fact, she writes that even though her "father was clean-shaven and George MacDonald was bearded," the two men "overlapped" in her life.[5] The characters in *The Princess and the Goblin* and *The Princess and Curdie* were similarly present in her consciousness; she explains that Curdie, the princess, and "the wise old woman who lived at the top of a flight of stairs that was not always there" were "totally real" for her (L'Engle, "Heroic," 121). Their influence, moreover, extends beyond that time and place. Since her empathic experience of burning when Curdie thrust "his hands into that extraordinary fire of roses," she, like him, could never consider a handshake, "merely a handshake," though she perhaps lacks his power to discern a person's character through that simple act (L'Engle, "Nourishment," 114). One has to wonder, too, about the influence of that fire of roses on Madoc's fire of flower petals in *A Swiftly Tilting Planet,* an image that—as she, of course, recognizes—goes back to Dante and perhaps beyond.

As she talks about her reading, L'Engle emphasizes its value in offering a world distinct from the world of school. "If I was intellectually starved at school, and sometimes pyschologically abused," she notes, "I was nourished at home in my own little room" (L'Engle, "Nourishment," 114). Though her school experiences did not begin that badly, they soon became psychologically destructive. She enjoyed her work and her teachers in her first three years at school, but then her mother, over her father's objections, enrolled her in a private school for girls. The young Madeleine, however, felt alienated from peers and teachers alike. She was set apart from the other students because of her clumsiness at athletics, which were very important at that school. She was estranged from her teachers by their lack of sensitivity and understanding. L'Engle recalls that one teacher apparently decided that her ineptitude in athletics indicated that she "wasn't very bright" and so would ignore or ridicule any creative or academic work that she would do. Moreover, in an incident that L'Engle claims revealed to her "the perfidy of the adult world," another teacher refused to allow her to go to the bathroom, but after she had wet her pants and complained to the principal, the teacher denied Madeleine's story and accused her of lying.[6] She was understandably miserable in this new school, but her father, with a perverse sort of logic, insisted that because her mother had made the decision, Madeleine had to remain there.

As difficult as these experiences were at the time, their value lay in the effect they had in shaping L'Engle as a writer. They forced her to develop a rich interior world, and they provided the material for a significant portion of her fiction. Writing became her means of processing hurt, and this period of pain gave her much to write about. "I built up a body of work," she acknowledges, "that I never would have done if I had been happy and popular with my peers" (Fox and Jacobs, 12). Such experiences, no doubt, inform the difficulties that Meg and Charles Wallace Murry have with their peers and teachers, but they are more explicitly related to the boarding school experiences of Philippa Hunter and Katherine Forrester.

Those fictional characters are also based, in part, on L'Engle's own ordeal in boarding school, which, she notes, "continued the hell that school had been for me" (L'Engle, "Nourishment," 117). In an effort to find clean, dry air for her father, who was vulnerable to pneumonia, L'Engle's family rented a château in Publier in the French Alps. The château had not received many improvements since the eleventh century, and while being without a stove, refrigerator, and running water was probably a shock for her parents, L'Engle enjoyed the summer "dreaming and wandering through the dusty rooms of the château" (*Two-Part,* 7). But that romantic exploring soon ended when L'Engle was sent to an Anglican boarding school in Switzerland. In her naïveté, L'Engle "hoped that the school would be a continuation of the dream" of Madeleine, "daughter of the château," but she found that the experience was anything but romantic.[7] The atmosphere of the school was legalistic and regimented. Students were referred to by numbers, and the crisply uniformed matrons were suspicious of girls spending time alone. Bathrooms were routinely checked; baths were closely monitored; even the chapel was watched. L'Engle was once pulled from there by her ear, "as though," as she wryly puts it, "going to be with God was something obscene and perverse" (L'Engle, "Nourishment," 117). Such rigidity and suspicions figure significantly in the plots of *And Both Were Young* and *A Small Rain.*

Again, although L'Engle chafed against the strict routine of the school, she credits the experience with contributing to her artistic sensibility. That contribution, of course, was not a deliberate offering of the boarding school; instead, it was a result of L'Engle's response to her environment. Because of the lack of privacy, L'Engle learned intense concentration. She learned, she says, "to shut out the sound of the school and listen to the story or poem" she was writing in the place of doing her studies (*Summer,* 100). This skill was one that she was able to sustain so that she later could write while touring with a play and that she can now write while traveling to and from speaking engagements.

While at this school, L'Engle also discovered the richness of her subconscious by paying close attention to her dreams. She and her school partner planted poppies in the school's garden plot in the hope that the poppies would yield opium which, they believed from reading *Fu Manchu* and *Bulldog Drummond,* would inspire wonderful dreams. The two girls "ate poppy-seed sandwiches, poppy-flower sandwiches, poppy-leaf sandwiches" and kept notebooks under their pillows to record their dreams (*Summer,* 101). While L'Engle soon determined that she did not need to eat poppies to dream, she does credit this experience with awakening a sensitivity to the world of the subconscious, a sensitivity that is crucial to her as a writer.

While L'Engle was in school in Switzerland, her parents lived in a variety of rented accommodations, from villas to pensions to small hotels, and the period was not any easier for them than it was for her. L'Engle's father's health did not improve and her mother's was delicate. Consequently, when L'Engle was 14, the family returned to the States, moving in with L'Engle's maternal grandmother in her beach house in northern Florida, a place which lies behind the settings of *Ilsa* and *The Other Side of the Sun*. The transition to American culture was something of a shock. L'Engle explains that she "was totally unprepared for a world in which girls wore bras and makeup and conversation was about dates" (L'Engle, "Nourishment," 118). Her experience of such cultural dissonance perhaps gives shape to the similar social contrasts that Polly O'Keefe feels upon moving from an island off Portugal to an island off the Carolina coast.

Thus it was that when she was sent to another boarding school—this one Ashley Hall in Charleston, South Carolina—she was relieved to be going to another girls' school. Here, she reports that "for the first time" she "was happy in school"; here, she "was appreciated and a leader" (*Two-Part,* 10). In fact, during her senior year, she edited the school's literary magazine and acted successfully in leading roles in school plays. Her happiness over her success at Ashley Hall—comparable to that experienced by the character Polly at Cowpertown High in *A House Like a Lotus*—was soured somewhat, however. That year, L'Engle's father died, pushing her to ask hard questions about death and suffering that she would address repeatedly in her fiction later on.

Her college years extended the positive experiences that began for L'Engle at Ashley Hall. She thinks of them as "good" years, explaining that during her time at Smith College, she "did a great deal of growing up," a fair amount of it being painful. Though by her own admission she "cut far too many classes," she also did manage to write "dozens of short stories" and "to get an excellent education despite myself" (*Summer,* 101). The sense of independence that was developing all through her education continued as she graduated from Smith in 1941. Although some of her family thought that she should return to the South to care for her mother, L'Engle knew exactly what she wanted to do, and that was not it. "After college," she relates, "I headed like a homing pigeon for New York. It was the place of my birth. It was where I would find music and art, theatre and publishing; it was where I belonged" (*Two-Part,* 12).

In New York, she found what she was looking for. Within five years, she had acted on Broadway, published a well-received novel, and married Hugh Franklin, a very successful stage actor most remembered for his later portrayal of Dr. Tyler on television's *All My Children.* She met Franklin while both were in the traveling company of a production of Anton Chekhov's *The Cherry Orchard.* Just prior to the first rehearsal of that play, L'Engle had completed work on what was to be published as *A Small Rain,* a novel that combines some of her boarding school experiences with her postgraduate life in New York as well as with some of the events connected with her first acting job on Broadway—an understudy's role in *Uncle Harry* with Eva Le Gallienne and Joseph Schildkraut, two famous actors of the period.

Stepping out professionally and entering into marriage both required consideration of names. Consequently, in the mid-1940s, Madeleine L'Engle Camp became Madeleine L'Engle. She dropped her father's name when she published her first novel because she wanted to make it on her own, with her own name, not on the influence of his name in publishing circles. The surname *L'Engle,* which also seemed to her to be a "more felicitous" name for a writer than *Camp,* was taken from her mother's side of the family, a branch whose history enters some of the fiction, most notably *Dragons in the Waters.* The decision to assume her baptismal name was not an easy one. It was wrenching for her, and her mother questioned whether in changing her name she was rejecting her father. A year or so after making the decision, she married Franklin, and while she then was willing to change her name to his, her publishers urged her to retain her own because of the "good start" she had established as Madeleine L'Engle (*Summer,* 110).

Soon after the marriage, L'Engle and Franklin bought a two-hundred-year-old farmhouse in northwest Connecticut, a house that was to become a symbol of their marriage and their family life as well as the setting that lies behind many of the scenes and adventures of the Austins and the Murrys. The house, Crosswicks, named after the village in which L'Engle's father spent his youth, is near L'Engle's own starwatching rock. It is where their children, Bion and Josephine, played and began school, just as the Austin and the Murry children would. It is where their adopted daughter, Maria, came to live with them after the death of her parents, just as Maggie came to live with the Austins. Indeed, the surrounding fields and trees and the atmosphere of Crosswicks seem to be very much a part of the novels, from the warm kitchen of *A Wrinkle in Time* to the pastoral scenes of *An Acceptable Time*. Yet if the settings and events of the fiction are sometimes colored by the life of L'Engle's family at Crosswicks and elsewhere, she adamantly asserts that her characters are not based on her family. "I would not presume to write out of my children," she declares. "My protagonists, male and female, are me."[8]

For most of the decade of the 1950s, L'Engle and Franklin lived exclusively at Crosswicks, and for a time they ran the local general store. The decade was a difficult one for L'Engle, who was trying to be a full-time mother and a writer. She wanted to make her husband and her children her first priority, but she also wanted to make her writing her first priority, as well. The effort to do both was exhausting. "There I was," she recalls, "absolutely stuck in bucology, with the washing machine freezing at least once a week, the kitchen never above 55° when the wind blew from the northwest, not able to write until after my little ones were in bed, by which time I was so tired that I often quite literally fell asleep at the typewriter."[9] It was, she explains, "probably my most unhappy decade. I had several books published before this time, and had recently begun to realize my work was God's gift to me and I was God's servant." Yet during those years she received "countless rejections," and she sold "only two stories and one novel."[10]

Around 1960, L'Engle and her family decided to move back to New York. The summer prior to the move the family went on a cross-country camping trip, an adventure that is translated into fiction in *The Moon by Night*. In fact, when an early draft of the novel was read to them, L'Engle's children complained that some of the narrative was too close to reality—too close to their mother's journal account of the trip—so L'Engle threw away the draft and began again. It was during this trip, interestingly enough, that L'Engle got the idea for *A Wrinkle in Time*. As her family was driving down the highway, the names of the three ladies—Mrs. Whatsit, Mrs. Who, and Mrs. Which—materialized in L'Engle's mind, and she knew that she wanted to write a book about them.

After she wrote the novel, however, publishers were not as impressed with the idea as she was. They wanted to know if it was for children or adults, and most did not accept L'Engle's response that it was for *"people"*—that "people read books" (Donahue, 45). When the novel was finally published it was a great success, winning the Newbery Medal in 1963, and as L'Engle looks back on the years in which it was rejected she wonders if the public would have been ready for it when she wrote it, if, indeed, it would have been as popular if it had been immediately accepted by a publisher.

Her difficulties with publishers came, in part, from the fact that L'Engle believes that she has a responsibility as a writer to respond to problems in society and to deal with difficult matters like suffering and death, matters that publishers in the fifties and early sixties were slow to recognize as appropriate for young adults. She says that "A writer who writes a story which has no response to what is going on in the world is not only copping out himself but helping others to be irresponsible, too" (*Circle*, 98). Consequently, *A Wrinkle in Time* examines the implications of social conformity whether it be in Middle America or in a totalitarian state, and *The Young Unicorns* not only addresses some of the challenges that the Austins and L'Engle's family met in readjusting to urban life, but it also examines some of the reasons for gang violence and drug use.

Death, moreover, is a frequent topic of her books, because it is a frequent occurrence, and because writing about it is her way of working toward healing in her own life. The deaths of her father and mother, though decades apart, were significant events in her life. Besides, in that difficult decade when she was in her thirties, she and Franklin suffered the death of four of their closest friends within a period of two years. These, no doubt, and other bereavements inform her treatment of death in *Meet the Austins, The Moon by Night, A Ring of Endless Light,* and *A House Like a Lotus.* The hardest death of all, however, was that of her husband, Hugh, of cancer in 1986, and it is hard not to hear L'Engle's own voice when, in *An Acceptable Time,* Polly says to Zachary, "You don't get over someone's death. Ever. You just learn to go on living the best way that you can."[11]

Any reading of L'Engle's biography points to the importance she places on story for understanding the world. If, for her, writing is a way of living "creatively" rather than "fearfully," then it is as important to understand her ideas about fiction as it is to understand something of her life (*Walking,* 53). The lesson she had learned from her early reading was that if she "wanted to find out the truth, to find out why people did terrible things to each other, or sometimes wonderful things—why there was war, why children are abused—I was more likely to find the truth in a story than in the encyclopedia."[12] *Truth* and *story* are terms that are often connected when she discusses her writing because writing has come to be her way of trying to answer those kinds of difficult questions, her way of expressing her optimism and faith in a world in which it is difficult to have either. But for her, story is more than just expression and more than just answering questions, even if they are hard ones; story is our culture's "most sacred possession, just as it is for the "Bushpeople" of the Kalahari, and "it is up to all of us to keep it alive."[13]

This view of story is one reason that L'Engle writes for young adults; they still possess the potential to exercise optimism and faith. She knows that because young people have not moved fully into the adult culture, they have access to a vision of reality that is broader than an adult vision because it is untainted by cynicism. She echoes both Jesus and William Wordsworth in asserting that "only the most mature of us are able to be childlike" (*Walking,* 74). Indeed, when she expresses such a faith in youth, she is speaking both as a Romantic and as a Christian. "We all have glimpses of glory" when we are young, she writes. However, "as we grow up we forget them, or are taught to think we made them up; they couldn't possibly have been real, because to most of us who are grown up, reality is like radium, and can be borne only in very small quantities." (*Walking,* 64). L'Engle asserts that because of their naive faith and their lack of acculturation, young people are more open to what she terms reality. "Sometimes," she writes, "if I have something I want to say that is too difficult for adults to swallow, then I will write it for" young adults because they "haven't closed themselves off with fear of the unknown, fear of revolution, or the scramble for security. They are still familiar with the inborn vocabulary of myth" (*Circle,* 198–199).

Many of L'Engle's novels are fantasies, and her commitment to that genre comes in part out of her desire to preserve this inborn language of myth in young people. In her view, this commitment runs counter to mainstream educational interests, which in their empirical emphases are equipping young people to function in a limited world using the outdated paradigms of Euclidean geometry, thus "keeping from them the vast open reaches of the imagination that led Einstein to soar out among the galaxies" in his quest for truth (*Circle,* 203). But for her, fantasy is not simply an exercise for the imagination, something "that should be discarded for reality as soon as we come of age."[14] Rather, fantasy serves as "a search for a deeper reality, for the truth that will make us more free" (L'Engle, "Fantasy Is," 130). A realistic literary vision is not adequate to the realities of the universe. If, she writes, "our universe is expanding out into space at enormous speeds," then "too our imagination must expand as we search for the knowledge that will in its turn expand into wisdom, and from wisdom to truth" (*Circle,* 203).

Here, too, L' Engle's notion of truth is clearly theological. "The fantasies," she says, "are my theology."[15] What she means by this, however, is not conveyed in the ordinary connotations of the word *theological,* but in its literal meaning of *words about God.* Though they are not systematic or rational after the manner of conventional theologies, the fantasies offer her a literary vehicle for apprehending the mysteries of God in the universe. Such an imaginative vision, such "creativity opens us to revelation" (*Walking*, 75). Such a vision sees angels and unicorns, the possibility of other worlds and the mysticism of theoretical physics as being as much a part of God's revelation as the birds of the air and the trees of the field. What she seeks to do in her fantasies is what in her view all mythic writers do—"to affirm that the gods are not irrational, that there is structure and meaning in the universe, that God is responsible for his creation" (*Circle*, 205). That is what she says she was trying to do in *A Wrinkle in Time*, which, for her, "was a very theological book" because in it she "was writing about a universe created by a God of love" (Donahue, 45).

For L'Engle, any theory of story must include a theory of cosmology. "One cannot discuss structure in writing," she asserts, "without discussing structure in all life; it is impossible to talk about why anybody writes a book or paints a picture or composes a symphony without talking about the nature of the universe" (*Circle*, 62–63). Still, her cosmology is not so pat as her statement about a responsible God might suggest. The universe is "a world of randomness, of chance," and the challenge of living in such an "open and undetermined universe" is to face it with a spirituality characterized by "courage and grace."[16] "Courage and grace" here really mean a kind of existential Christian faith, for the cosmological options that L'Engle sees are three. We can "live life as though it's all a cosmic accident"; we can live life as though it were controlled by an impersonal "prime mover"; or—and this is her way—we can "live as though [we] believe that the power behind the universe is a power of love, a personal power of love, a power so great that all of us really *do* matter to him," that is, God (*Circle*, 63–64). The connection between cosmology and story comes in the fact that "the artist's response to the irrationality of the world is to paint or sing or write, not to impose restrictive rules but to rejoice in pattern and meaning, for there is something in all artists which rejects coincidence and accident" (*Summer*, 14).

The work then stands as an icon of creation; in its mimicry of the structure of Creation, it more than points toward the Creator, it recreates some of His essence. A sign, according to L'Engle, points the way toward something, but a symbol "contains within it some quality of what it represents" (*Walking*, 28), and an icon is a symbol rather than a sign. But an icon is not necessarily literally mimetic in its attempt to portray its subject, and neither is a story. The distinction is somewhat similar to Nathaniel Hawthorne's distinction between romance and fiction; the former, like an icon, deals with "the truth of the human heart," whereas the latter treats the "probable and ordinary course of man's experience."[17] When a book functions as an icon, it offers us a "glimpse of the truth, that truth which casts the shadows into Plato's cave, the shadows which are all we mortals are able to see" (*Circle*, 61–62).

In an age in which writers are given to belittling the significance of their fiction, this is a rather high view of story. But in talking about story, L'Engle uses language that is even stranger to the contemporary ear. Her theory reflects her Christianity as much as it does her romanticism or affinity with Plato. Story is a gift, not from the Muse, but from God, and a gift from God requires obedience. "The artist," she writes, "must be obedient to the work" just as Mary was obedient in the Annunciation (*Walking*, 18). When the work says, "Here I am: compose me, or write me; or paint me," the duty of the artist "is to serve the work" (*Irrational*, 122). Writing stories, then, or engaging in any artistic creation is a religious activity. "As I understand the gift of the spirit in art, so I understand prayer," writes L'Engle, "and there is little difference for me between praying and writing. At their best both become completely unselfconscious activities; the self-conscious, fragmented person is totally thrown away and integrated in work" (*Irrational*, 122).

This view of story necessarily emphasizes the value of intuition in the writing process. Because the reality that L'Engle attempts to apprehend in her fiction surpasses empirical reality, she seeks to write with more than just her intellect. "When I try to grasp the nature of the universe with my conscious mind, my humanly limited intellectual powers, I grope blindly," she writes; however, she feels that she comes "closer to understanding with the language of the heart" than when she thinks "with the mind alone" (*Irrational*, 4). Her goal is not for "intellectual understanding," but for "a feeling of rightness, of knowing, knowing things which we are not yet able to understand" (*Walking,* 23). Part of serving the work, then, is following the direction it takes, even if that runs counter to what the intellect would suggest. L'Engle talks of listening to the book, just as she listens in prayer. "If the book tells me to do something completely unexpected," she notes wryly, "I heed it; the book is usually right" (*Irrational,* 160).

Such obedience, particularly obedience to the dark impulses of intuition, might seem a curious commitment for a Christian writer. And, indeed, it does intially sound more like the pledge of an anti-Christian Romantic in the tradition of William Blake or Percy Bysshe Shelley. Yet L'Engle perceives it as necessary to a right perception of Creation. She takes evil seriously, and she recognizes that evil sometimes appears under the guise of good, that, as she repeatedly reminds readers, the devil often masquerades as an angel of light. In fact, the plots of the books in the time trilogy are built to some degree on that assumption. In addition, she draws on the traditional Christian dichotomy between light and dark throughout her fiction. The good characters, the namers, serve the light; the evil characters, the destroyers, serve the dark. But she is not willing to extend that analogy to the human psyche if it means that reason should triumph over intuition because reason is imagistically related to the light and intuition is imagistically related to the dark. She insists that "all the things which we have shoved down into the darkness of the subconscious were created to be good." Indeed, "The darkness itself is good, but we have distorted so many things within it that the Destroyer has taken it over and made it a power for evil, for the breaking and destruction of God's creatures" (*Irrational,* 203). The risk of entering "the deep black waters of the subconscious mind" is genuine, she admits, but so is the reward. That intuitive darkness is "that part of us which is capable of true prayer, poetry, painting, music"; it is only by entering it that any of us "have any hope of wholeness" (*Irrational,* 202).

Although for some writers the dive into the "waters of the subconscious" leads to a theory of narrative that is almost exclusively autobiographical, L'Engle's plunge yields somewhat different results. She draws on the "underwater treasure trove." "I can swim," she writes, for example, of a particular summer of her childhood, "for hours beneath the surface; or I can bring up a shell, a piece of coral, up into the sunlight" (*Summer*, 90). Yet instead of focusing the narrative as an exploration of the autobiographical experience, she simply mines it as a tool to develop a character or to advance a plot. This use of the subconscious requires a function of memory that she labels "anamnesis," a function that enables her to write out of her "child self":[18]

> When I am writing in a novel about a fourteen-year-old girl, I must remember what I was like at fourteen, but this anamnesis is not a looking back, from my present chronological age, at Madeleine, aged fourteen. If there is all this distance of years between us, my memory is only from the outside. When I am writing about a fourteen-year-old girl I will not succeed unless I am, during the time of writing, Madeleine: fourteen. The strange wonder of it is that I am also Madeleine: fifty-seven, with all the experience I have gained in the intervening years. But I am not, in the ordinary sense, remembering what it was like to be fourteen; it is not something in the past; it is present; I am fourteen. (*Irrational*, 16–17)

L'Engle is present, then, in a great many of her characters. As her husband, Hugh, once noted, "If Meg Murray and Vicky Austin have bits and pieces of the young Madeleine L'Engle, their mothers have large chunks of the mature Madeleine Franklin."[19] Yet her presence extends beyond the mothers and their daughters, for parts of her inhabit characters like Charles Wallace, Grandfather Eaton, Adam Eddington, Uncle Douglas, and even Gaudior and Proginoskes.

Perhaps the most significant autobiographical influence on L'Engle's fiction is her faith, for though she "resists the reputation of being a 'Christian writer,'" she most certainly is, in the language she prefers, "a writer who is a Christian" (Fox and Jacobs, 4). Whereas, in her view a "Christian writer" might be concerned about mentioning the name of Jesus a requisite number of times or might feel obliged to avoid a type of incident or language that was ugly, a "writer who is a Christian" might not mention Jesus and might employ ugly incidents or language. Her rationale for choosing the latter is twofold. First she has the confidence that her faith will, if genuine, shine through her art. She writes that "what we are is going to be visible in our art, no matter how secular (on the surface) the subject may be" (*Walking,* 122). Second, she perceives the mission of all Christians to be evangelical, concluding, nonetheless, that her mission is not to alienate non-Christian readers by antagonizing them. "We do not draw people to Christ," she argues, "by loudly discrediting what they believe, by telling them how wrong they are and how right we are, but by showing them a light so lovely that they want with all their hearts to know the source of it" (*Walking,* 122). Even so, L'Engle feels that many in the world of publishing have little respect for her faith; she observes that it seems spiritually chic to be a Sufi or a Druid, but not to be a Christian.

Paradoxically, however, this light that L'Engle seeks to shine apparently has antagonized Christian audiences more than non-Christian audiences. Throughout her career, she has been under almost continual challenge from Christians over what they perceive as the heresy of her beliefs. There have been those who have asserted that "Mrs. What, Mrs. Who, and Mrs. Which were witches practicing black magic."[20] There have been those who accuse her of universalism, a belief that every person in the universe will be saved, regardless of his or her belief in Jesus Christ.[21] There have been those who have accused her (as well as C. S. Lewis in the "Narnia Chronicles") of writing pornography (L'Engle, *Dare,* 16). There have been those who have indicted her inclusion of what they classify as "occult practices": "telepathy" and "the use of runes, scrying, astral travel, psychic healing, and the use of a medium with a crystal ball."[22] And there have been those who label her as a New Age spiritualist with an emphasis on the Bible as story and her belief that God can be perceived in all parts of creation.[23]

Most of these challenges have come from what L'Engle terms "the extreme evangelical right" (Fox and Jacobs, 5), a fragment of the Christian population that has little patience for someone who confesses that "it is not easy for me to be a Christian, to believe twenty-four hours a day all that I want to believe" (*Walking*, 106), who says , in fact, "if I 'believe' for two minutes once every month or so, I'm doing well" (*Summer,* 142). She terms herself "a Christian agnostic" because, though she cannot "know" God, she can "choose to 'believe'" what she does not "know."[24] For L'Engle faith includes an "acceptance of doubt" as opposed to "the repression of doubt," an acceptance that in her mind rests on the essential mystery of God; "doubt is part of faith because what I believe in is so incredible and so marvelous that how can I believe in it all the time?" (Fox and Jacobs, 15). Her critics hear this as a celebration of disbelief, when, in actuality, this stance reflects a humble realism, for the evidence of her work bears testimony to a stronger faith, a faith that is passionate and sincere. L'Engle herself acknowledges a connection between her work and her faith. "I have often been asked if my Christianity affects my stories," she confesses, "and surely it is the other way around; my stories affect my Christianity, restore me, shake me by the scruff of the neck, and pull this straying sinner into an awed faith" (*Walking,* 106).

The doctrinal issue that most frequently raises the ire of Christian critics is that of her alleged universalism. Again and again, the question arises after her lectures or in the middle of interviews. Her response is that she isn't a universalist, that she is, instead, "a particular incarnationalist," who "can understand God only through one specific particular, the incarnation of Jesus of Nazareth" (Forbes, 18). This, response, however, is not exactly clear, for while some of her comments say "no" to universalism, others say "yes." She seems to be saying "no" when she responds that she does not believe "that God, for no particular reason, is just going to wave a magic wand and say, 'Ok, everybody out of hell. Home free,'" when she says unequivocally, "I am not a universalist. I do not believe in playing trivially with free will" (L'Engle, *Door,* 24). But she seems to be saying "yes" when she remarks that "it's seductively pleasant to think that God loves Christians better than Buddhists or Hindus," when she questions those churches that "are holding adamantly to a heaven for Christians only."[25] Is she saying "no" when she says that she doesn't mean "to water down my Christianity into a vague kind of universalism, with Buddha and Mohammed all being more or less equal to Jesus" (*Walking,* 32)? Is she saying "yes" when she says that "to be truly Christian means to see Christ everywhere" (*Walking,* 32)?

At the root of the confusion is L'Engle's emphasis on the loving nature of God. She cites with favor the comment of George McDonald, her literary mentor, that "I did not care for God to love me if he did not love everybody" (L'Engle, "Nourishment," 115). For this reason, she takes Jesus' promise in 6 Matthew seriously. "If every hair of my head is counted," she asserts, "then in the very scheme of the cosmos I matter; I am created by a power who cares about the sparrow, and the rabbit in the snare, and the people on the crowded streets; who calls the stars by name. And you. And me" (*Circle,* 99–100). This sense of God's love for his whole Creation leads her to believe that, in her words, God is not "going to fail with creation" (Forbes, 24):

> God is not going to abandon Creation, nor the people up for trial in criminal court, nor the Shiites nor the communists nor the warmongers, nor the greedy and corrupt people in high places, nor the dope pushers, nor you, nor me. Bitter tears of repentance may be shed before we can join the celebration, but it won't be complete until we are all there. (*Stone,* 61)

For God to fail, for him to damn part of creation, would mean that Satan and not Christ had the victory over death. The Day of Judgment will not be a forensic judgment, a judgment of criminals: "The judgment of God is the judgment of love, not of power plays or vindication or hate" (*Stone,* 117). Because the whole Creation groans, the whole Creation will be redeemed, "not just the small portion of the population who have been given the grace to know and accept Christ. All the strayed and stolen sheep. All the lost little ones" (*Stone,* 117).

If L'Engle's theology is confusing here, perhaps it is so also because of her unwillingness to limit God in any way. Language, imagination, science, and theology all are inadequate to capture the essence of God. Her God—"the only God worth believing in"—is neither her "pal on the house next door," nor "an old gentleman shut up in a coffin" where he is safe. Rather, he is "the *mysterium tremendens et fascinans,*" a God not easily explained (*Summer,* 142). To L'Engle's eyes the story of much of theology has been one of reductive miscomprehension; ever since God appeared to humanity, he has been misunderstood and limited by those to whom he has appeared, in part because "we're afraid of the unsheathed lightning; our binding him with ropes of chronology instead of trying to understand his freedom in *kairos.* Not that we've done any of this to the Lord himself, only to our image of the One we worship, and that's bad enough" (*Irrational,* 157). If this respect for God's ineffable nature sometimes leads L'Engle to make statements that are theologically troubling for some in her audience, such respect is, nonetheless, at the center of her theory of story.

Her stories are her response to this God of mystery; they are her response of obedience and her attempt to understand this God and the wonderful, yet baffling universe that he created. Her stories raise questions: "What is this universe like? What are its possibilities? How deep is space? Why is there so much suffering? What does it mean? What if—" (*Walking,* 135). Her questions are not pat ones; they are questions that probe reality, questions that essay her faith—questions of the nature of God and the nature of evil, questions of love and questions of pain. "The questions worth asking," she writes, "are not answerable." But that is exactly her point in asking them. "Could we be fascinated by a maker who was completely explained and understood?" she asks. The pull of story is the pull of the unknowable: "The mystery is tremendous, and the fascination that keeps me returning to the questions affirms that they are worth asking, and that any God worth believing in is the God not only of the immensities of the galaxies . . . but also the God of love who cares about the sufferings of us human beings and is here, with us, for us, in our pain and in our joy" (*Two-Part,* 123). Thus, for L' Engle, the writing of stories is ultimately an exercise of faith, but that exercise inevitably produces friction with some readers because, as she notes, "every new question is going to disturb someone's universe" (*Dare,* 23).

Writing fiction, then, for L'Engle, is not merely a way of ordering life, it is a way of living it. The choices before a storyteller as she composes are the same spiritual and moral decisions that any individual confronts daily. The effect that a writer has then also bears moral consequences. "Like it or not," L'Engle asserts, "we either add to the darkness of indifference and out-and-out evil which surrounds us or we light a candle to see by" (*Circle*, 99).

2. Quests in Time

When I was pushing forty, living in a two hundred plus year old farmhouse, trying to raise three young children, to write, to cope with rejection slips, I asked again all the cosmic questions I had asked as a teenager. I wasn't finding help in any of the expected places.

Then, by some chance, I'm not sure how or why, I stumbled on a book of Einstein's, in which I read that "any one who is not lost in rapturous awe at the power and glory of the mind behind the universe is as good as a burnt out candle," and in Einstein I found my theologian. From then on I have found my deepest theology in reading about particle physics, quantum mechanics, astrophysics, because these disciplines are dealing with the nature of the universe.

"Kerlan Award Lecture," 1990

L'Engle was trying to exercise her visionary storytelling when she wrote *A Wrinkle in Time,* and so she was troubled when her vision did not translate into publication.[1] For more than two years this novel—the first of what has come to be known as the Time Trilogy—was rejected by publisher after publisher, and at the time the rejection caused L'Engle to question her vocation. Since God was her muse, she yelled at him in the midst of receiving her more than 40 rejection slips: "God, why all these rejection slips?

You know it's good; I wrote it for you" (Donahue, 1990). Yet when one of her mother's friends introduced her to John Farrar of Farrar, Strauss, & Giroux at a Christmas party, her book did find a publisher. The acceptance kept L'Engle from eschewing the vocation of writing for that of homemaking, and it gave readers the first in what was to be a remarkable series of fantasy fiction. Even then the publishers did not expect the book to succeed, and so they were surprised when *Wrinkle* went on to win the Newbery Medal in 1963 and to become so popular internationally that it has been translated into 15 languages.

The stars of the series are the Murrys, the ordinary and extraordinary family that populates the plots of *A Wind in the Door* and *A Swiftly Tilting Planet,* as well as *Wrinkle.*[2] Mr. Murry is a physicist who works for the fictional equivalent of NASA, and Mrs. Murry is an experimental biologist who, working out of a lab in their rural home, manages to be a nurturing mother as well as a ground-breaking scientist. The family has four children: the twins, Sandy and Dennys, who are athletic and socially successful; Meg, who is bright but misunderstood and who has trouble socially, and Charles Wallace, who is precocious and who has telepathic gifts. Meg and Charles Wallace function as the dual protagonists of the trilogy, but their identities are firmly grounded in the Murry family, and the family is never too far in the background. In that way, the novels point to the value of family bonds even as they celebrate the importance of individual actions. Even though the family is ordinary, if somewhat idealized, in its social interactions, it is extraordinary in its high concentration of unusually gifted individuals. Using such a cast of scientifically and intellectually talented characters in the early sixties was somewhat extraordinary as well, and L'Engle has been praised for her creation of strong female characters.[3] Making Meg a protagonist, for example, "opened the door for many more female protagonists in recent science fiction," according to one critic.[4]

Though they are all inhabited by the Murrys, the novels stand by themselves even while they complement the others in the group and so, as Gary Schmidt has pointed out, the novels are an "integrated series" as opposed to "a traditional trilogy like that of

J. R. R. Tolkien, where the conclusions of the first two novels leave so many things open that they might not properly be called conclusions."[5] The plots, however, use similar archetypes in a number of ways. Each presents a character on a quest that is circular as opposed to linear: here the hero does not fulfill the quest by traveling from point A to point B; instead, "the hero escapes from the normal world as defined by home and society, into a fantasy world where he undergoes experiences that ultimately allow him to return to the normal world a more self-confident, knowledgeable, and adjusted individual."[6] Moreover, in each quest, the protagonist (or protagonists) is guided to the fantasy world by some sort of spiritual being, what one critic terms "a psychopomp, a role generally played by an angel in Christian thought."[7] Like angels, these guides can only aid the hero in identifying the purpose of the quest, in transporting the hero to particular otherworldly sites, or in proffering general advice about how to proceed in a particular adventure along the quest. The ultimate responsibility for the success of the quest rests with the hero, and therein lies the key to the plots of these novels. Each places the hero in a conflict between good and evil, a battle or series of battles with significant consequences for the hero both in the fantasy world and in the real world. Each focuses on the importance of selfless and responsible moral action, action based on faith or love, action that typically carries great danger for the actor.

Each of the quests, too, moves freely throughout time and space in what constitutes L'Engle's effort to express "a vision of hope." She draws on Einstein's theory of relativity, Max Karl Ernst Ludwig Planck's Quantum theory, and her own theory of time to craft narratives that find a pattern in the "seeming meaninglessness" of events.[8] L'Engle asserts that there is "a difference between ordinary time, or *chronos,* and God's time, *kairos,* which is real time."[9] In *kairos,* notions of past and present are irrelevant; characters in what we might think of as an earlier chronological time can have an awareness of the future, and characters in what we might think of as the present can affect "prior" events. Since in L'Engle's view, "An artist is free to know *kairos,*" (Forbes, 19), she is also free to employ those glimpses of eternity in her fictions. Significantly, the term itself comes from a Greek word that appears in the Bible in instances when the author wants to indicate that a given time offers an especially opportune moment to change or to act in accordance with God's will. L'Engle moves her protagonists through *chronos* to demonstrate the possibilities of *kairos,* and each quest brings a bit of what L'Engle sees as eternal truth.

On their journeys, those characters discover the importance of humility, interdependence, and responsibility. They learn L'Engle's version of heroic behavior, a mode of action that requires relinquishment of pride and control. She believes that

> honorable behavior is possible only where we are aware of our own lacks, where we understand that we are fragmented creatures . . . that we cannot control what is going to meet us around the corner, or how the day is going to end. The only way I can accept my own impotence to control my life and the world around me is to walk into the future with a child's simplicity, and a child's awareness of interdependence. (L'Engle, "Bird," 273)

To hold such faith, however, is not to face the world with passivity, for coupled with the humility is responsibility. These characters learn that even the smallest right action bears consequences in the battles in which they find themselves, a phenomenon that L'Engle would later identify as "the butterfly effect." This "beautiful and imaginative concept" from astrophysics postulates that the death of a butterfly on earth "would be felt in galaxies thousands of light years away" (*Stone,* 42).

A Wrinkle in Time

Meg Murry's quest in *Wrinkle* is an exploration of individuality and conformity, of good and evil. The dragons she must slay are in one sense projections of her own mind—her insecurity, her sense of inferiority, her misconceptions of the nature of reality. Physically, she ends the novel where she begins—the place is the same and the time is even the same, thanks to the miracle of the tesseract, the ability to travel through time and space, to "wrinkle" in time. Yet psychologically, she is a very different person, someone who no longer sees the world as she did at the outset of the narrative.

The "dark and stormy night" on which that narrative playfully begins follows what has been for Meg a less than perfect day. That day, however, filled as it was with misunderstandings and inequities, seems to her to be an apt metaphor for her life. Like many adolescents and, indeed, like a great many protagonists in adolescent fiction, she sees life as terrible and unfair. Her teachers misunderstand her, and "she'd been dropped down to the lowest section in her grade" (*Wrinkle,* 3). Her peers tease her for her "immature" behavior, and when they ridicule Charles Wallace, who is in reality a genius, as her "dumb baby brother" she fights on his behalf (*Wrinkle,* 4). She feels plain and awkward, a genetic aberration in the midst of an otherwise attractive and talented family. But the greatest problem of all is the absence of her father. Not only does she miss him greatly, she also burns with embarrassment and anger at the malicious gossip of teachers and townspeople about his disappearance. At the start of the novel, everything gives Meg a sense of otherness and she would like desperately to be "O.K." Her sense of alienation prompts in her a fierce desire for normalcy.

Meg's quest, then, is to address this problematic reality. What she wants is a quick fix, and as the adventure begins she keeps looking for it. She wants to understand reality; like most young people, she wants to find her place in the world. But one of the first lessons that she has to learn is to be comfortable in not knowing everything. For example, when she meets Calvin O'Keefe who, like Charles, is something of a telepath and who, unbeknownst to Meg, will be one of her companions on the quest, she immediately wants to know what to make of him. Her mother, wisely, urges her to be patient; to accept Calvin for who he is. Meg's challenge, as she tries to comprehend her father's disappearance or as she tries to understand who she is, is to have faith that reality is not always what it seems to be. She needs to learn what her mother already knows, that "just because we don't understand doesn't mean the explanation doesn't exist" (*Wrinkle,* 43). That challenge is a significant one for her because it entails her acceptance of who she is—of both the good and the bad—and her rejection of the community's opinion of her, and such self-awareness does not come easily.

L'Engle sends Meg, together with Calvin and Charles Wallace, to an alternate reality to engage the dragons of her quest, but she does not send them without help. The heroes are transported through space and time by three rather eccentric guardian angels—Mrs. Whatsit, Mrs. Who, and Mrs. Which—who set Meg's personal quest in a cosmic context, and show the young adventurers that their goal of retrieving Mr. Murry has implications far beyond the family. His disappearance is tied to a battle between forces of good and evil that are waging war for the entire universe, a battle that, as one critic notes, is "steeped in the classical and Gospel-of-John traditions."[10] Father is one of the reasons for the quest, but, the three ladies explain, "he's only one" (*Wrinkle,* 59). On the planet Uriel, the guardian angels show the questers a vision of the universe that is obscured on earth. They see a shadowy manifestation of evil that seeks to envelop stars and planets within its power, a shadow that represents ultimate evil. "What could there be," Meg thinks upon her first glimpse of this force, "about a shadow that was so terrible that she knew there had never been before or ever would be again anything that would chill her with a fear that was beyond shuddering, beyond crying or screaming, beyond the possibility of comfort" (*Wrinkle,* 68).

Still, Meg's horror is intensified upon the discovery that this force has partial control of the earth, that this force holds her father prisoner and that, therefore, it is this force that she must face. But the angels do not only show her evidence for despair. They also reveal the essence of the good, the beauty of a planet untainted by the "black thing": the creatures of this planet are engaged in a musical dance that can only be translated as a psalm of praise to the creator, a psalm that L'Engle takes from Isaiah 42:10–12.

> Sing unto the Lord a new song, and his praise from the end of the earth, ye that go down to the sea, and all that is therein; the isles, and the inhabitants thereof. Let the wilderness and the cities thereof lift their voice; let the inhabitants of the rock sing,

let them shout from the top of the mountains. Let them, give glory unto the Lord! (*Wrinkle, 64)*

Though Meg does not realize it at the time, this vision of the good provides her with a hint of the weapon that will give her victory in her quest—love. The joy that Meg experiences upon witnessing this scene prompts her instinctively to reach for Calvin's hand (*Wrinkle,* 64). The good brings people and, in this fantasy world, *creatures,* into communion together, and the bond of that communion is love.

Evil offers at best only a superficial replication of that kind of communion. The world of Camazotz, the dark planet on which Mr. Murry is trapped, is a world of uniformity. All behavior on this planet, named after a "malignant Mexican deity . . . worshipped as a vampire, a death bat, a preying creature of darkness," is controlled by a disembodied brain called IT (Stott, 35–36). Some readers have objected that this "too glibly suggests certain similarities between the cosmic struggle against evil and the Cold War," that the totalitarian world "is not so much a planet as a bogeyman—an early sixties American image of life in a Communist state."[11] And indeed, the planet, with its identical gray houses and its people that perform simultaneous actions "like a row of paper dolls" (*Wrinkle,* 99), does appear to comment on communist society, if not on the burgeoning American suburbia. But to insist on this historical reading of the novel is to miss the psychological significance of the planet for Meg and to belittle the dramatic function of the planet in the narrative of her quest.

The world of Camazotz is analogous to the small-town world that Meg has left, and she must deal with this logical extrapolation of her desire for conformity in order to complete her quest and return to that world. To mature and become self-aware, Meg needs to examine her subconscious desire for everything to fit together neatly, for everything to be all right. Because it parodies such desires, Camazotz provides Meg with the opportunity for such reflection. What is missing on Camazotz is what was also missing in her community—love. In explanation of the townspeople's misunderstanding of Mrs. Murry's sustained devotion to her husband despite "common sense," Calvin assures Meg that "they can't understand plain ordinary love when they see it" (Wrinkle, 48).

When she sees the parody of conformity on Camazotz, Meg immediately recognizes its wrongness, but her recognition is not the same as conscious rejection. She recognized some of the wrongness of the pressure toward conformity in her hometown as well yet, at least subconsciously, she wanted to conform. Her quest, therefore, requires her to confront evil in all its seductive malignity and persuasive power and to reject it. Speaking through Charles Wallace, whom IT has possessed, IT emphasizes the attraction of conformity to Meg. "On Camazotz we are all happy," he says, "because we are all alike" and he reminds her that the reason she is not happy at school is because she is "different" (Wrinkle, 134). The seduction of this incarnation of evil is that it is based on the truth. The possessed Charles is in one sense correct in his analysis of some of earth's problems. "Why do you think we have wars at home?" he asks Meg. "Why do you think people get confused and unhappy? Because they all live their own, separate, individual lives" (Wrinkle, 135).

Yet as seductive as the words of IT are, L'Engle uses setting and characterization to make clear the fact that it is, nonetheless, essentially perverse. The mechanized sterility and the architectural uniformity of the city on Camazotz serve as constant reminders to Meg of the ramifications of IT's seductive logic. But beyond that is the abrupt transformation of Charles Wallace's character. She only has to take note of his marionette-like gait, his pedantic voice, and his new insensitivity to see the effects of Camazotzian conformity. Thus, when Charles argues that there is no suffering or unhappiness in this utopia, Meg can counter that "nobody's ever happy either" (Wrinkle, 136).

Meg's resistance forces IT to try to conquer her by violence, by a kind of cerebral rape. Just when Meg realizes that "IT was getting at her," that "she, too, would be absorbed in IT," L'Engle jerks her to safety albeit on Ixchel, another unknown planet, via her father's inept tessering (Wrinkle, 155). But this section of the novel has troubled critics. This escape from IT requires that Meg confront IT again to complete her quest, and as they consider this penultimate encounter with IT together with the climactic one, critics have faulted L'Engle both for her narrative strategy and for her philosophical presentation of evil. Carolyn Horowitz, for example, cannot understand why Meg could not have resisted IT and saved Charles Wallace in the penultimate confrontation instead of the ultimate one,[12] and William Blackburn argues that in putting the characters in confrontation with IT, L'Engle simplistically "insists on seeing evil as something external to the human psyche" (129).

Yet the two scenes are vital to Meg's development. If L'Engle had allowed Meg to resist IT *à la* Horowitz's wishes or if she had sent one of the three Mrs. W's to rescue Meg *deus ex machina,* then Blackburn would be correct in his criticism. But L'Engle brings Meg to Ixchel to force her to look within herself, to recognize in her selfishness a taint of the same evil that animates IT and the Black Thing. In fact, even here, Meg initially resists self-examination and attempts to locate evil outside herself. Expressing disappointment that the narrator tells us "was as dark and corrosive in her as the Black Thing" (*Wrinkle,* 165), Meg blames her father. Caught up in self-pity, she gives up hope. All her previous hope had hinged on finding her father who, she believed, would do what fathers are supposed to do—solve all her problems. When she sees his limitations she lashes out at him:

"You don't even know where we are!" she cried out at her father. "We'll never see Mother or the twins again! We don't know where Earth is! Or even where Camazotz is! We're lost out in space! What are you going to *do!*" (*Wrinkle,* 165–66)

The evil that L'Engle portrays here is not a simplistic external evil. Both Meg and Charles Wallace are flawed by the presence of a more subtle force. This scene functions to demonstrate to the reader that evil is not merely external, as Meg would like to believe. L'Engle asserts that Meg is motivated by an internal evil that has possessed her, just as the evil that is behind IT has possessed Charles Wallace.

Meg is encouraged to look inward by her experiences on the planet Ixchel, named, significantly, "after the Maya Goddess of the Rainbow, the symbol of fecundity, [and] patron of the art of medicine" (Stott, 37). The planet lacks visible light and its inhabitants lack eyes; instead, they "see" with love, "looking" not at "temporal" things, but at "eternal" things (*Wrinkle,* 179). Through conversation with them and with the three Mrs. W's, Meg is compelled to look inward, and when she does, she sees what she could not see before. "I wanted you to do it all for me," she confesses to her father, "I wanted everything to be easy and simple" (*Wrinkle,* 193). She confesses her own complicity, her awareness that she blamed him out of fear and self-pity, and it is by making that confession of her internal motivations, as well as by loving and allowing herself to be loved by the creatures and by her companions, that Meg is healed.

But as she is healed she is also armed for her quest. Each of the three Mrs. W's presents Meg with a gift that she can use upon her return to Camazotz, but the gifts are not the gifts of conventional wisdom, but of the paradoxical wisdom of Christianity. Mrs. Whatsit gives Meg her love. Mrs. Who, who always speaks in quotations, gives her a snippet of St. Paul's Epistle to the Corinthians, a text that offers empowerment to the weak:

> The foolishness of God is wiser than men; and the weakness of God is stronger than men. For ye see your calling, brethren, how that not many wise men after the flesh, not many mighty, not many noble, are called, but God hath chosen the foolish things of the world to confound the things which are mighty. And base things of the world, and things which are despised, hath God chosen, yea, and things which are not, to bring to nought things that are. (*Wrinkle,* 194)

This gift represents an apparent shift in L'Engle's intention in *Wrinkle.* In an earlier draft of the novel, she has Mrs. Who offer a much more ethereal gift by quoting Henry David Thoreau: "Time is but the stream I go a-fishing in. . . . I would drink deeper, fish in the sky whose bottom is pebbly with stars."[13] The "foolishness" that Mrs. Who commends to Meg complements the final gift of the supernatural trio. Mrs. Which gives Meg her only weapon, something that Meg must discover for herself, but something, according to the angel, that IT does not have (*Wrinkle,* 195).

That weapon, of course, is love, and L'Engle not only makes Meg discover it, but she also makes Meg figure out how to wield it as a weapon. In part, L'Engle puts Meg under this pressure because such discoveries of power are part of the conventions of the quest narrative. But L'Engle also has philosophical reasons for making Meg sweat. L'Engle strongly believes in the human freedom of choice. She avoids, then, anything that would smack of determinism. Life, she believes, is like a sonnet—structured, but not determined. As Mrs. Whatsit tells the children, "You're given the form, but you have to write the sonnet yourself. What you say is completely up to you" (*Wrinkle,* 192). On Ixchel, Meg had learned about love, but to complete her quest, to be mature, she has to face evil directly and put what she has learned into action.

When Meg discovers that love can break the bonds of evil, her quest is complete, for the love that she has discovered is a love that can set her free just as it released Charles Wallace from the power of IT. The love she finds is deeper than the superficial love of popular culture; it is stronger than the romantic love that attracts her to Calvin; it is more powerful than the fraternal love that bound her instinctively to Charles Wallace and her father in the earlier confrontation with IT. The love she finds is the selfless love of agape, for she finds it in the events on Ixchel where she is loved despite her faults and where she acknowledges her responsibility to risk her life to love Charles Wallace the same way. Equipped with such a love, a love that gives her the assurance that she need not conform in order to be "good," Meg is ready to reenter reality. No chronological time has passed on earth, but she is a changed person, confident enough of who she is to face social difficulties she might meet. Her quest is over.

A Wind in the Door

The challenge that Meg faces in *A Wind in the Door* is exactly the challenge that Meg was left with at the conclusion of *A Wrinkle in Time*—that of exercising this love in the community. This time her quest has three parts; in each she must affirm a person or creature that is difficult to affirm. L'Engle's term for this kind of exercise of love is *naming*, a concept which is of great importance to her. To name someone is to affirm that individual in all his or her peculiarity, to love that person despite his or her flaws. Yet in the terms of this novel, this naming is much more than an exercise in potential realization therapy. The business of naming is part of a cosmic struggle between good and evil that has consequences both for the universe and for the Murry family. L'Engle makes each ordeal of Meg's quest increasingly difficult in order to emphasize the necessity of self-sacrifice to the exercise of love. If in *Wrinkle,* Meg learns something of moral responsibility and agapic love, in *Wind* her lesson is completed. Whereas some reviewers initially complained that *Wind* was more "philosophical" than its predecessor, most agreed that it successfully created a highly unusual world of fantasy.[14]

But L'Engle did not have such grand plans for this story originally. She wrote an earlier version of the fantasy as a short story called "Intergalactic P.S. 3."[15] This story, published in pamphlet form in 1970 for Children's Book Week, is very much a light sequel to *Wrinkle.* The conflict that initiates the plot is Murry's concern for Charles Wallace's schooling; they are afraid that he just will not fit in with normal first graders. Consequently, Meg signals the three Mrs. Ws who enroll Charles along with Meg and Calvin in a school on another planet—Intergalactic P.S. 3. Some of the other students are related to creatures that the trio met in their adventures in *Wrinkle*—"small versions of the beautiful creatures from Uriel; the strange, tentacled, eyeless beasts from Ixchel" (*Intergalactic,* 14). Others are creatures that readers will recognize from *Wind*—Proginoskes attends, as does Sporos, though he is a perky conifer seed instead of the arrogant microscopic creature that he is in *Wind.* Meg's lesson is much the same as her first test in *Wind;* in a metaphysical version of a 1960s television game show, she has to pick out the correct Mr. Jenkins— the school principal that so misunderstood her in *Wrinkle*—from a group of three identical men. As in *Wrinkle,* the lesson carries cosmic consequences, but in this story, those consequences do not carry much emotional weight. Whereas in *Wind,* a mistake in Meg's decision will harm Proginoskes, Charles Wallace, *and* the universe, here the sole repercussion is that the mistake will be "a victory for the Dark Shadow" (*Intergalactic,* 35). Consequently, the lesson carries little power, and the story offers little beyond entertainment.

But the changes L'Engle makes as she converts this story into a novel transform it from a diverting sequel that is dependent on the reader's memory of *Wrinkle* to a powerful novel that is related to *Wrinkle* but that stands on its own. As one reviewer has noted, the novel is "a completely convincing tale that should put under its spell both readers familiar with the Murrys and those meeting them for the first time" (Murray, 8). L'Engle reshapes the materials that she used in "Intergalactic P.S. 3" so that the characters are more fully developed and the problem of the novel is more complex. Nonetheless, the skeletal plot of the new novel is similar to its predecessor. Once again, a female protagonist, Meg, is aided by a pyschopomp—here, Proginoskes, a cherubim—in fighting a cosmic battle. Once again, the pyschopomp can offer only limited aid; the quest is Meg's. And once again the quest in the fantasy realm is designed to equip Meg to live in the real world.

Once again, too, L'Engle begins the novel with an alienated protagonist. But unlike the alienation that Meg feels at the start of "Intergalactic P.S. 3," this alienation is authentic. Whereas in the short story Meg's concern was for anticipated trouble, here her concern comes out of actual problems. The Murrys simply do not quite fit in with their neighbors in their rural community. The townspeople gossip about them. Charles Wallace has gone to school for two months, and there has not been a week in which he has not been roughed up by other school children. To make matters worse, Meg's parents do not intervene on his behalf, and when Meg takes it upon herself to be Charles Wallace's advocate before the principal, Mr. Jenkins, she only brings trouble on herself. But what really disturbs Meg is the state of her younger brother's health. The slightest exertion causes him to perspire and breathe heavily, and as the novel begins, he seems to have lost touch with reality. When Charles Wallace reports that he has seen a drive of dragons, Meg wonders whether she is becoming alienated from her brother, too. The realistic presentation of Meg's emotions in the early chapters positions readers to identify with her as she faces her quest.

That quest is a spiritual one, and to understand the quest, we need to comprehend the spiritual danger, a dimension of the novel that is strongly developed. "No one," observes one critic, "can match Miss L'Engle's treatment of the powers of darkness."[16] The problem is a kind of personified nihilism, an active evil that is attacking the universe by convincing creatures to deny their importance in a symbiotic creation. The manifestations of the attack are manifold. On the cosmic level, stars, contrary to Einstein's Law, seem to be annihilated, causing a "small rip in the galaxy" (*Wind*, 37). But, as Mr. Murry observes, "it isn't just in distant galaxies that strange, unreasonable things are happening. Unreason has crept up on us so insidiously that we've hardly been aware of it" (*Wind*, 85). On a cultural level vandalism, violence, and environmental abuse are escalating. On the microscopic level, farandolae, experimentally postulated subunits of mitochondria, the cellular energy organelles, are destroying their mitochondrial and human hosts, and Charles Wallace is one such host. Behind the attacks of macrocosm and microcosm are Ecthroi, fallen angels that go about the business of war and hate. Their method, Proginoskes informs Meg, "is un-Naming—making people not know who they are. If someone knows who he is, really knows, then he doesn't need to hate" (*Wind*, 98).

Meg's quest is to counter the Ecthroi by Naming the people or creatures she encounters in each of her ordeals. "That's why we need Namers," Proginoskes tells her, "because there are places throughout the universe like your planet Earth. When everyone is really and truly Named, then the Ecthroi will be vanquished" (*Wind*, 98). Naming people in the midst of a spiritual battle is not, however, a light matter for Meg. In every case there is considerable risk to herself and to individuals that she cares for. In fact, L'Engle fashions these scenes to highlight Meg's existential risk. To name someone else, Meg has to take a leap of faith, to jeopardize much that she values.

The first test introduces Meg to the essentials of Naming. When she is confronted with three manifestations of Mr. Jenkins, she discovers the difficulty of Naming. "A Namer," Proginoskes tells her, "has to know who people are, and who they are meant to be" (*Wind*, 97). Meg's difficulty is that she views Jenkins stereotypically. To her, "no matter how many Mr. Jenkinses there were, he was Mr. Jenkins. That's all" (*Wind*, 99). He was the small-minded, ineffectual principal who harassed her, and so she wonders aloud, "How do I Name Mr. Jenkins when all I think of when I see him is how awful he is?" (*Wind*, 99). Proginoskes' answer is crucial to L'Engle's theme. He tells Meg that she has to love Jenkins.

To do that, Meg needs a lesson in love, a lesson that highlights the existential dimension of agapic love. In this scene, Meg learns that the exercise of this kind of love, though it carries tremendous risks, endows life with meaning and that to avoid the exercise of love because of fear strips life of meaning, granting victory to the Ecthroi. The stakes of the contest are high. A wrong choice will put Charles Wallace at greater risk and will force Proginoskes to choose between annihilating himself and going over to the enemy. But the high stakes only cloud Meg's discernment until she learns the most important lesson about love—that love is action, not emotion. "Love isn't how you feel," the cherubim tells her, "It's what you do" (*Wind*, 118). And by stepping back from her feelings for Jenkins, Meg is able to see his flaws as foibles and to love him in his imperfection.

The second ordeal of Meg's quest takes the group into a somewhat unconventional fantasy realm. The "teacher" who has introduced the questers to the quest—one Blajeny—transports the group to Metron Ariston, which is neither another planet, nor another dimension in the typical science fiction sense. Instead it is a "postulatum" which "makes it possible for all sizes to become relative." Here, Blajeny tells them, "you may be sized so that you are able to converse with a giant star or a tiny farandola" (128). Here, the questers converse via kything, L'Engle's version of mental telepathy. This realm has been criticized for being "too confusingly vague"[17] and "too fantastic to have any usable connection with reality."[18] But it is precisely the vagueness of Metron Ariston that permits a merging of macrocosm and microcosm that is essential to *Wind*'s theme of interdependency.

The term *kything* is one that L'Engle discovered in an old Scottish dictionary of her grandfather's "to express this communication without words, where there is 'neither speech nor language.'" Although it is analogous to extrasensory perception, it is, in L'Engle's view more than that. "It goes much further," she says, "for it takes a deep faith in the goodness of creation and the power of love to open oneself in love and hope and faith."[19] Those additional elements of faith and trust are very much evident in the subsequent ordeals that Meg faces.

L'Engle's shaping of the second ordeal emphasizes the uniformity of the evil that attacks the whole universe. It simply is not true that "L'Engle's metaphor fails to bridge the distance between the real and the symbolic experience" (MacCleod, 101). On the contrary, if anything, the scene is too anthropomorphic. L'Engle makes the problems of the farandolae exactly the problems of humanity—pride and hedonism. Sporos, the farandola that inhabits a mitochondrion in Charles Wallace's body sees himself as superior to his human host. When told that humans were not convinced about the existence of farandolae, he is astonished: "It's a very stupid breed of creature that doesn't know its own inhabitants. Especially if it's fortunate enough to be inhabited by farandolae. We are extremely important and getting more so" (*Wind*, 137). Sporos is so self-absorbed that he can assert that the importance of "earthlings" consists in the fact that "they are inhabited by farandolae" (*Wind*, 139), but readers will note that such self-absorption is also a very human characteristic.

Ironically, in the world of the novel, Sporos is correct about the importance of farandolae, but one reason for that increased significance is the arrogance of his generation, an arrogance that values self-gratification more highly than the fulfillment of its biological function. The hedonism is the source of the mitochondritis that is threatening Charles Wallace. The normal biological pattern for a young farandola like Sporos is to "deepen." As an immature creature, Sporos is shrimplike and can swim at will within the world of the mitochondrion; however, to mature—to deepen and become an energy-producing constituent of the mitochondrion—he must plant himself in the wall of the mitochondrion. Though such deepening seems limiting to the immature Sporos, it actually is expansive. The process really functions as a metaphor for the paradox of Christianity; just as, according to Christian doctrine, an individual must die to self in order to experience the fullness of life in God, Sporos must let go of his immature identity to know the fullness of his mature identity. As L'Engle explains the process through Progonoskes, we learn that deepening will remove Sporos's need "to run about": "A grown fara is less limited than a human being is by time and place, because farae can be with each other any time in any place" (*Wind,* 155). But for farandolae, as well as for humans, the Kirkegaardian leap of faith is difficult. "The temptation for farandola or for man or for star," as Proginoskes explains, "is to remain an immature pleasure-seeker. When we seek our own pleasure as the ultimate good we place ourselves as the center of the universe." In L'Engle's view, each creature has its place, "but nothing created is the center" (*Wind,* 178).

The lesson of the second test is self-sacrifice. When Sporos and his generation of farandolae listen to the Ecthroi, denying their function, dancing instead a "savage, wild, furious" dance, the questers need to intervene. The Ecthroi have taught the farandolae that nothing matters, and they have believed. "We don't need to Deepen," they say. "That's only an old superstition. It's a stupid song they sing, all this Glory, glory, glory. We are the ones who are glorious" (*Wind,* 189). As the scene comes to a climax, some of the farae are dying, and the questers realize that the only way of halting the madness and saving Charles Wallace is by filling the void of the Ecthroi. And so, first Meg and then the others throw themselves into the void. When she does, Meg finds her own life being sucked from her to sustain the dying farandola, until Mr. Jenkins embraces her and sustains her with his love and strength. His intervention breaks the crazed, destructive dance of the farandolae. As in the first test, love brings victory over evil, but here the stakes are higher; here, the exercise of love necessitates the hazarding of self.

The third and final test combines the lessons of the first two, for in the process of saving Sporos, Mr. Jenkins has been captured by the Ecthroi and is possessed by their nihilistic reason. "It is not the Ecthroi who are empty," he says; "it was I. They have filled me with the pleasure of the abyss of nothingness" (*Wind,* 197). To save Jenkins, Meg has to name him again, but this time she has to risk her self, "kything herself entirely to him" (*Wind,* 199). The challenge is too much for her as she slips impressionistically into nothingness:

> Cold.
> Darkness.
> Emptiness.
> Nothing.
> Naught.
> Nought.
> Ecthth
> X (*Wind,* 201–202)

She is saved from annihilation only by Proginoskes's annihilation of himself in her place.

The cherubim's sacrifice lends Meg the strength to name the Ecthroi as well as all the distinctive components of the universe. She sings a song of epiphany, a song that is part of the music of the spheres:

> I Name you, Ecthroi. I Name you Meg.
> I Name you Calvin.
> I Name you Mr. Jenkins.
> I Name you Proginoskes.
> I fill you with Naming.
> Be!
> Be, butterfly and behemoth,
> be galaxy and grasshopper,
> star and sparrow,
> you matter,
> you are,
> be! (*Wind,* 203)

The song names much more, and the theme is clear. Significantly, the mitochondrion in which Sporos has deepened is named Yadah, a Hebrew word for praise that is used in biblical Psalms. Once more, Meg is back where she began, but what she has learned is the message of this psalm—the incredible importance of being. This is the lesson of the ordeals, that through love, through self-sacrifice, a person can become more fully herself. Meg's lesson is one in ontology, in being. Elsewhere, L'Engle writes that "the part of us that has to be burned away is something like the deadwood on the bush; it has to go, to be burned in the terrible fire of reality, until there is nothing left but our ontological selves; what we are meant to be" (*Circle,* 7). At the end of *Wind,* Meg's quest is completed and Charles Wallace is saved, but she is changed. The ordeals have burned away her selfishness and her fear, and she is content simply to be.

A Swiftly Tilting Planet

Like the first, the third novel in the series begins on a dark and stormy night, but from there L'Engle takes the plot in a very different direction. The cast of characters is the same; there *is* travel through time and space; and there *is* a quest, but the quest is different in that L'Engle divides it between Charles Wallace and Meg. Married to Calvin and pregnant with their first child, Meg supports the 15-year-old Charles Wallace on the quest, but she accompanies him only through the ties of their kythe.

This alteration in the plot from the pattern of the first two novels might seem to remove *Planet* from the series, but it does not. Despite, or perhaps because of, this variation in the plot, L'Engle works hard to keep Meg in the reader's mind as a youthful protagonist, and her efforts reinforce the bond between this and the prior novels. In fact, in an early draft of the novel, L'Engle experimented with giving Charles Wallace a more prominent role emotionally by emphasizing his loneliness, a strategy that in that draft bonds him with the unicorn who is also a lonely figure.[20] Yet in the published version, L'Engle does not offer readers that kind of emotional attractiveness. Instead, with Calvin away in Europe, L'Engle places Meg in her old bedroom, and has her revert to former habits. In a development that would have to delight the young adult reader who has identified with Meg in *Wrinkle* and

Wind, the narrator tells us that Meg "looked like a child again," albeit "a far lovelier child than she actually had been" (*Planet,* 29). Because she is pregnant, her overly protective family treats her like a child, warning her again and again to take care of her cold, to get sleep, to drink milk, and Dennys observes that she looks as though she is 15 years old (*Planet,* 101). She behaves that way, too, rehearsing old signals with Charles Wallace, criticizing herself for "settling for the grownup world" (*Planet,* 49), and reverting to her youthful "habit of talking out loud to the family animals" (*Planet,* 43). Because of the emphasis on her youthful manner, it is difficult to imagine Meg as anything but a slightly more confident version of the Meg that we have met before. Her presence in the novel certainly is not an adult presence.

This youthful Meg never leaves the Murray house, but as she kythes with Charles Wallace who is traveling through time and space, she serves as a reflector of the action. This strategy, while it sustains continuity with the other narratives in the series, renders *Planet* somewhat less engaging than *Wrinkle* or *Wind.* The narrative is strikingly complex; the reason, no doubt, for the American Book Award and for some critics' assessment that "L'Engle's gifts are at their most impressive here."[21] Yet the appeal of the narrative is intellectual rather than emotional; the characterization does not invite emotional identification with either Meg or Charles Wallace. Instead, the plot stimulates curiosity about the impact of the quest on world events. Charles Wallace may be more than the "passive, if uniquely present, onlooker" that one reviewer termed him, but he is not a hero with whom readers can easily identify. Similarly, although it may be true that "Meg's role is even more passive and less engaging," she certainly does more than alternate "between wringing her hands in the family kitchen and stroking a strange dog on her attic bed while fretfully following Charles Wallace's adventures in her 'kything' mind."[22] Though L'Engle's characterization here does not establish psychological bonds with the reader in the way that it does in her other novels, she does establish a kind of intimacy with the reader through the use of dramatic irony. Because Meg reflects the action and because she is kything with Charles Wallace, she gives readers knowledge of the adventure that the other Murrys do not possess. As one critic suggests, "we kythe with the narrator and Meg as she kythes with Charles Wallace."[23]

The plot seems to begin as a realistic narrative that is going to explore contemporary political issues, the "tilting" of the title. The Murray family has gathered for a Thanksgiving dinner when their peace is shattered by a telephone call from the president of the United States seeking Mr. Murry's scientific advice in a foreign policy crisis. Mad Dog Branzillo, dictator of Vespugia, a small country in South America, has issued an ultimatum to the United States. The dictator is threatening nuclear war to punish the superpower. L'Engle places Mr. Murry on a kind of soapbox as he explains "El Rabioso's" perspective. The dictator's complaint, Mr. Murry proclaims, is with America's gluttony. The U.S. and the Western world have disproportionately consumed the earth's resources and are responsible, therefore, for the world's environmental crisis.

But the novel does not remain realistic for long. L'Engle interjects Calvin O'Keefe's mother into the plot to establish the fantasy dimension of the narrative. The idea for doing so came as something as a surprise to her; she recalls that when she was "blocking out" the novel, "Calvin's slovenly mother rather unexpectedly appeared in the first chapter, giving Charles Wallace" what she calls Patrick's Rune and charging him to stop Branzillo (L'Engle "Heroic," 124). The rune itself, which calls upon the natural elements to battle the powers of darkness, came to L'Engle on a card from a friend right at the time she was struggling to discover a structure for the novel, and L'Engle decided to use its catalog of the elements as a structural motif for the novel:

> I place all heaven with its power
> And the sun with its brightness,
> And the snow with its whiteness,
> And the fire with all the strength it hath,
> And the lightning with its rapid wrath,
> And the winds with their swiftness along their path,
> And the sea with its deepness,
> And the rocks with their steepness,

And the earth with its starkness,
All these I place
By God's almighty help and grace
Between myself and the powers of darkness! (*Planet*, 269)

The Murrys quickly discover that when spoken the rune employs one or more of the elements to hinder the cause of evil. When Mrs. O'Keefe presents the rune to the family, the power and lights go out, the fire in the fireplace dwindles, and an odor like the stench of the Ecthroi fills the room. But when the rune is uttered, a bolt of lightning apparently destroys the power of darkness, restoring light and power to the house.

But even such a powerful rune proffers little obvious aid in halting nuclear war, and L'Engle intends nothing that melodramatic or oversimplified. Instead, it is merely a tool that Charles Wallace uses as he travels though time and space on his quest accompanied by his guide or psychopomp, a unicorn named Gaudior, a Latin term meaning "more joyful" (*Planet*, 46). The quest, which is shaped to develop L'Engle's themes of interdependency and of the significance of responsible action, takes Charles Wallace into the past in the hope that action there will alter the future. Gaudior explains his task as a search for the particular actions that have led to the contemporary nuclear threat:

> But there is always a moment when there is a Might-Have-Been. What we do is find the Might-Have-Beens which have led to this particular evil. I have seen many Might-Have-Beens. If such and such had been chosen, then this would not have followed. If so and so had been done, then light would partner the dark instead of being snuffed out. It is possible that you can move into the moment of a Might-Have-Been and change it. (*Planet*, 55)

As the quest takes them into the past, Charles Wallace is to "go within" significant individuals to attempt to alter the Might-Have-Been. The drama of the novel comes in the ways that the powers of darkness seek to disrupt this quest and to turn these Might-Have-Beens to the worse.

At the heart of the quest is an archetypal conflict between two brothers, two Welshmen who, like Cain and Abel, possess opposite temperaments and in the world of the novel offer very different legacies to future generations. The one—Madoc, with blue eyes and the gift of crystal gazing or scrying—abhors violence, eschews power, and works for peace. The other—Gwydyr, with dark eyes and no visionary powers—embraces violence, covets power, and pushes for war. Each of the historical episodes that Charles Wallace seeks to alter involves a conflict between these two lines, and in each Charles Wallace goes "within" a descendant of Madoc's line in an attempt to sway events toward the good, while the powers of darkness employ a descendant of Gwydyr to effect the opposite reality. L'Engle uses Patrick's Rune to order these episodes; the chapter titles derive from the lines of the rune, each focusing on a different element, and at the climactic moment of each episode, one of the characters employs the rune to rescue the quest or to save Madoc's line. The names of some of the characters come from Welsh legend; others, like *Harcels* and *Llawcaes* are formed from rearrangements of *Charles* or *Wallace*.

Following similar dramatic patterns, each of the episodes moves Charles Wallace closer to the goal of the quest by altering a bit of history and preparing him for the next test. In the first, he gets his initial glimpse of the two versions of reality. Through Madoc's gift of scrying he receives a hint as to how this historical interference might affect the twentieth-century crisis. In a puddle of water, Madoc sees two visions. The first is of Branzillo, the dictator, as a baby:

> Madoc saw a black-haired woman holding and rocking the baby. "You shall be great, little Madog," she said, "and call all the world your own, to keep or destroy as you will. It is an evil world, little Madog." The baby looked at her, and his eyes were set close together, like Gwydyr's, and turned inward, just so, and his mouth pouted with discontent. (*Planet,* 92)

The vision concludes with images of a nuclear holocaust, and although Madoc does not know what he is seeing, Meg and Charles

Wallace do, and so they have reason to hope at Madoc's second vision:

> "No more of Gwydyr's nightmares," he commanded, staring fixedly at the water, which sparkled from the sun. The water rippled and shimmered and resolved itself once again into a mother holding a baby, but a different baby, eyes apart, with sunlight gleaming through the blue, a laughing merry baby. "You will do good for your people, El Zarco, little Blue Eyes," the mother crooned. "Your eyes are an omen, a token for peace." (*Planet*, 94)

In this second vision, L'Engle reveals the genealogical objective of the quest—to alter history sufficiently so that El Zarco will replace El Rabioso.

L'Engle shapes the second episode to position Madoc's descendants a step closer to Vespugia but also to take a subtle jab at her religious critics. The episode is set in the seventeenth-century on the spot where the Murry home will be some centuries later. Here Madoc's descendants sustain their relationship with the People of the Wind, the Indian tribe that originally adopted Madoc, only to find that relationship and their lives endangered by Gwydyr's descendants who appear in this incarnation as puritanical Christians. Suspicious of the Native American religious practices and of the gift of second sight, the Christians accuse Madoc's descendants of witchcraft. The wrongfully narrow-minded accusations and censorious mob psychology echo the charges of occultism and pornography that various groups brought against L'Engle after the publication of *Wrinkle* and *Wind*, and the implied identification of such critics as power-hungry descendants of Gwydyr is, in the terms of this novel, damning indeed.[24] But whatever L'Engle's intentions were regarding her critics, the episode furthers the plot by bringing Madoc's line closer to South America. Wounded by the charges of witchcraft, some of the family returns to Wales from whence they will later join a Welsh emigration to Patagonia.

Part of the danger Charles Wallace faces on the quest is a result of his own hubris. Just as in *Wrinkle* he has to learn that he can't attack IT in his own power, so here he learns the price of arrogance. It is a lesson that he learns the hard way. As the information he garners from the quest and from Meg as she kythes facts to him point to the importance of Patagonia, Charles Wallace insists on Gaudior trying to control the wind—the benevolent force that transports them through time and space—even though an earlier attempt at control had blown them into a projection—a perverse, alternative version of reality created by the Ecthroi. The attempt nearly kills both Gaudior and Charles Wallace, but it teaches Charles Wallace to approach the quest with humility. As he apologizes to Gaudior for his arrogance, he acknowledges that he has "learned that every time [he's] tried to control things [they've] had trouble," and he admits that in himself he is helpless to direct the quest (*Planet,* 160).

That lesson is crucial to L'Engle's thematic concerns. If the structure of the episodes points to the significance of individual actions, it also points to the importance of humility. Having learned this lesson, Charles Wallace is prepared for the last two tests of the quest, both of which will place him within a person with handicaps, situations that according to L'Engle call for heroic values that are often overlooked: "It was really important for me to learn that, in our society and particularly in our church, we are so dependent on our own version of strength. But Charles Wallace had to let it all go when he went into Chuck" (Schmidt, "Teller," 14). The self-negation and empathy required lead her to compare his action to intercessory prayer: "So when Charles Wallace limits himself to someone else's limitations, he is moving with compassion into somebody else's problems, letting his own go" (Schmidt, "Teller," 14). The Chuck that L'Engle refers to here is Mrs. O'Keefe's brother, a young boy who, while Charles Wallace is within him, is beaten by one of the twentieth-century descendants of the repressive puritans. Because of the resultant brain damage and institutionalization of Chuck, the wind takes Charles Wallace out of the situation, but the episode nonetheless establishes a link between the O'Keefe family and the South American dictator, and it builds reader sympathy for the O'Keefes.

In the final episode, Charles enters Matthew Maddox, a nineteenth-century American novelist who both weaves his own fictional accounts of the Welsh colony in Patagonia and conspires to alter that reality by sending the appropriate Welsh maiden to marry the appropriate Welshman to ensure the birth of El Zarco instead of El Rabioso. Yet even here, L'Engle creates a climax that emphasizes the importance of communal action more than it highlights Charles Wallace's successful manipulation of history. Just when it appears that all things may be well, Matthew Maddox falls ill and the kythe—the mental bond—between Charles Wallace and Meg is ruptured. The unlikely hero of this scene is Mrs. O'Keefe, who runs to Charles Wallace as he lies "eyes closed, white as death," obviously in great peril (*Planet,* 268). Together with Meg she utters the rune, throwing herself between the ailing youth and the powers of darkness, a scene that explodes heroic stereotypes.

All does end well, but the questers are the only ones who know it. Because history has been successfully altered, "El Rabioso was never born." Instead, we are told "It's always been El Zarco" (*Planet,* 277). As Charles Wallace analyzes his experience, L'Engle's theme is clear. He expresses his belief that, indeed, everything will be all right, but not because he "was intelligent, or brave, or in control." Moreover, he says, "Meg was right, earlier this evening, when she talked about everything, everywhere, interacting" (*Planet,* 273). To be heroic in L'Engle's world is to be willing to risk all to act on the behalf of others, and to do so with humility, conscious that every person has the same heroic burden and potential. To be heroic is to serve.

3. An Assurance of Things Hoped For

> I do not want ever to be indifferent to the joys and beauties of this life. For through these, as through pain, we are enabled to see purpose in randomness, pattern in chaos. We do not have to understand that order to believe that behind the mystery and the fascination is love.
>
> —*Two-Part Invention*

Imagine a family, a typical WASP middle-class family of the late 1950s or pre-counterculture 1960s. Imagine a physician-father who does not like women to wear pants and a mother at home who wears skirts to please her husband. Imagine two girls and two boys. Imagine a family that sings together, reads books together, even eats meals together and you have imagined the Austins—a family that inhabits six of L'Engle's books. If that leads you to imagine six rather conventional novels, you would be both right and wrong. Just as the Austin family is in one sense a typical American family, so the novels in which they appear are in one sense conventional adolescent fiction. For the most part, the books place a rather typical girl—Vicky Austin—in rather typical situations facing rather typical problems.

This is particularly true in the two Austin books that are really long short-stories—*The Twenty-four Days Before Christmas* and *The Anti-Muffins*.[1] In the first, we see a seven-year-old Vicky who is concerned about her role in the Christmas pageant, a role that is endangered both by the imminent birth of a sibling and by a threatening snowstorm. When the storm does cause the cancellation of the Christmas Eve service, that disappointment is tempered by the home birth of a baby brother, a birth that renews the joy of Christmas for Vicky and the family. In the second, *The Anti-Muffins*, a story written from sections cut from an early draft of *Meet the Austins*, a 12-year-old Vicky suffers the measles and all the Austin children form a club to celebrate their nonconformity with the uniformly molded "muffins" of their community. Both are realistic narratives that celebrate what have become known in recent social discourse as "family values"; in fact, *The Anti-Muffins* was published by the United Church Board for Homeland Ministries as part of a monograph series designed to aid discussion of moral values in public schools.

Yet at the same time the four major novels—*Meet the Austins, The Moon by Night, The Young Unicorns,* and *A Ring of Endless Light*—are much more than conventional, if by conventional we mean something akin to propaganda for the status quo.[2] They were certainly not perceived as conventional in their own time. L'Engle reports, for example, that publishers wanted to have nothing to do with *Meet the Austins* because it begins with a death. In fact each of the major novels in this group deals realistically with hard issues—death, drug abuse, the problem of evil itself. The novels seriously engage the problem of evil in ways that make the issue accessible to preadolescent or adolescent readers without trivializing it. Part of what makes the issue engaging to young adults is L'Engle's focus on Vicky Austin as she moves from preteen to teenager. This is a rather typical young person in rather typical situations—struggling with sibling rivalry, confused by adolescent restlessness, intrigued by emergent feelings of sexuality, tempted by peer pressure. Yet in each of these typical situations, Vicky and the other Austins have to come to terms with what L'Engle elsewhere terms "the irrationality of the world" (*Summer*, 14).

But what also works to make the problem of evil accessible is that the degree of sophistication with which L'Engle addresses it in each case parallels the developmental maturity of the protagonist. In *Meet the Austins,* the preadolescent Vicky learns to face a hurtful and confusing world by drawing on her family's strength and values. In *The Moon by Night,* the early adolescent Vicky feels the pull of competing values as she struggles with the problem while simultaneously struggling with matters of identity that put her in tension with the family. Though she ultimately is able to come to an acceptance of who she is without letting go of the family's faith, she finds that faith tested in *The Young Unicorns,* where L'Engle tries the viability of the family's faith in a broader social context. Finally, as an older adolescent in *A Ring of Endless Light,* Vicky formulates a personal faith with which she is capable of facing the problem of evil independently of her family.

L'Engle's treatment of these hard issues is intentional. She comments that young adults want to know about the unanswerable questions as well as the answerable ones, and that adults must not prevent them from asking just because we cannot provide pat answers. In asking unanswerable questions—in raising the question of death in *Meet the Austins,* for example—L'Engle was anticipating what has come to be known as the "new realism," in which young readers were permitted to experience areas of life and confront issues that were formerly taboo.

Meet the Austins

Meet the Austins opens with just such an unanswerable question: "Why do people have to die?" The narrative begins with a description of what "started out to be a nice, normal, noisy evening" with the smell of roast and the sounds of playing children pervading the country home of the Austins. But that warm scene is soon shattered by a telephone call announcing the death of a close family friend—Uncle Hal, a test pilot who with his copilot has been killed in a crash. The news shakes the children's world, for this is the death of an adult who, in 12-year-old Vicky's words, "wasn't nearly as tall as Daddy, but was sort of big and solid, like a rock," a man who "was so tremendously alive you couldn't imagine anything ever happening to him" (*Austins*, 11). To lose such an adult poses a threat to analogous adults in the children's lives. Vicky's comparison of Hal and her father is not accidental; children naturally draw such associations. In Vicky's mind, because her uncle has been killed, "suddenly, Daddy was in danger, too" (*Austins*, 15). To a young person, writes L'Engle in describing the incidents on which she based this novel, the parent "is still god," and the death of that parent represents a betrayal both of the young person and of the order of the universe (*Circle*, 114). Thus Hal's death strikes the children particularly hard; it violates what Erik Erikson identifies as the most basic stage of psychological development—trust, the assurance that everything is going to be all right.

The initial chapter of *Meet the Austins* realistically demonstrates the way that death shatters the security and normalcy of the children's world. First of all, Vicky and the others discover the limitations of parental power. Their mother can normally rectify any problem, but in this case there is simply nothing that she can do to change things. The breakdown in order extends to the relationships between the siblings as well. They attempt to carry on with normal routines, but unable to articulate their fears, they bicker, as in this exchange between Vicky and John, her older brother, when she is having difficulty bathing Rob, their youngest sibling:

> Then John came in and shouted at me, for heaven's sake, couldn't I think of Mother for once and do a simple thing like giving Rob his bath without causing all this sound and fury?
> I sat back down and I started to shout at John, but, instead, my voice sort of crumbled and I said, "Oh, John." (*Austins*, 13–14)

As her voice and her anger crumbles, Vicky, of course, realizes what we as readers already know—that the bickering is the result of misdirected anger at the death that has disrupted the family order. Through a number of similar incidents, L'Engle employs dramatic irony to help her readers feel the emotional climate brought on by the shock of death.

The issue that these young people face, however, is not just death; it is the larger problem of evil, the problem of facing an imperfect world where the inexplicable occurs. For them, that means facing change of all kinds. John articulates what the others perhaps are not mature enough to enunciate:

> Oh, Mother, why do things have to change and be different! . . .
> I like us exactly the way we are, our family. Why do people have
> to die, and people grow up and get married, and everybody grow
> away from each other? I wish we could just go on being exactly
> the way we are! (*Austins,* 37)

This concern with change represents an early adolescent response to an apparently unpredictable world, a recognition of mutability.

L'Engle's metaphor for change is Maggy, the orphaned daughter of Hal's copilot, who is dropped, as it were, into the Austin family. Her arrival is a consequence of death, and it forces the Austins to deal with change. Her presence serves as a catalyst for a primary aspect of the plot—the family's reaction to a mutable world. Maggy's character is based on one of L'Engle's daughters, Maria, who came to the family as "a legacy" from close friends who died within a year of each other, leaving "a seven-year-old girl, suddenly and unexpectedly orphaned" (*Two-Part,* 155). Like Maggy's, Maria's response to the upheaval in her life "was to test the cosmos" (*Circle,* 114). And so the chronicle of Maggy's arrival in the Austin house is a chronicle of disruption. She breaks rules and toys alike, and to Vicky and the rest of the family, "there seemed to be more Maggy than the rest of us put together" so that "no matter where you turned in the house, Maggy was always there" (*Austins,* 51).

Even if she could rationally accept the changes and the reality of having Maggy in the family, Vicky could not emotionally embrace that reality as easily. Instead, she attempts to blame Maggy for all her problems as well as her own impulses to misbehave. In the central chapter of the novel, Vicky meets with a day on which everything seems to go wrong. The family environment is disrupted by silly arguments and by the discovery of petty thefts committed by Vicky's younger sister, Suzy. Then after she has a terrible day at school, Vicky quarrels with John over his complaints about her piano playing and his accusation that she contributes nothing to the household. When she does attempt to do something—to bleed the radiators—her good intentions backfire as she breaks the radiator valve, causing it to spew water everywhere. Feeling completely misunderstood, she violates a household rule and bicycles to a friend's house after dark, only to fall and break her arm and seriously injure her face and jaw. All through this series of events she realizes her responsibility for them, and although rationally she knows that "this one I couldn't blame in any way on Maggy" (*Austins,* 85), she accedes to the impulse to do so. As she lies in the hospital bed she muses as she "lay there miserably, that before Maggy came to stay I'd never been as stupid and horrid and disobedient as I'd been that afternoon" (*Austins,* 85). Instead of acknowledging the evil within herself, Vicky at least temporarily tries to locate it outside herself, and since Maggy appears to her the most obvious variable, she is tempted to the logical fallacy of cause and effect.

Vicky's avoidance of responsibility is only temporary, but L'Engle shapes her repentance to illustrate how a young person can acknowledge failure and the problem of evil without being consumed by guilt. The key is in being honest and in having a supportive community—in this case, her family. When her father visits her in the hospital and offers her the opportunity to postpone discussing the incident, Vicky responds that she wants to get her confessions over with. Throughout her lengthy recounting of the events, Dr. Austin is stern yet sensitive to Vicky's emotional state. In his response, he reminds Vicky of her communal identity as a family member, telling her that she has been punishing herself more harshly than either of her parents would have, and apprising her of the fact that the sight of her injuries frightened the whole family. The effect of this speech is not to produce guilt, but to move Vicky firmly to a sense of responsibility that can be cathartic for her. By showing her love and by offering her a sense of the communal stability of family, Mr. Austin helps Vicky move beyond a kind of selfishness toward a more realistic interpretation of the events. When she says at the conclusion of the chapter that she does not suppose that they will know exactly why these incidents occurred, that she does not understand why the whole family acted terribly to Maggy instead of behaving the way in which they prefer to think of themselves, she is one step closer to where L'Engle wants her to be, to where she can see Maggy not as a problem, but as a person. In taking that step, Vicky has come to a healthier, more mature understanding of the nature of evil.

But part of the power of the novel's treatment of this issue is that Vicky's new vision does not make her safe from further trouble. Whereas a conventional treatment might reward the protagonist for her right decision, L'Engle's treatment does just the opposite. Just when she has begun to like Maggy and to accept her as part of the family, she is faced with another difficulty—the threat of her removal. Thus the stability of the family is threatened just as it was coalescing. Vicky notes that ironically she is not as glad as she thought she would be that Maggy will not be with the family much longer, and she and John berate themselves for pulling pranks on Maggy's relative who, without identifying her purpose, was making a surprise inspection of the family, an inspection in which the Austins did not pass muster. As they express their concern at this point in the events, their affection for their foster sister is evident, but the question of her safety and of the consequent security of the family is one that hangs over all of them for virtually the rest of the novel.

The novel's answer to the question of "why?" is to suggest that the proper response to the fear of the unknown is to look beyond oneself. This is evident in L'Engle's treatment of nature and in her characterization of the family's grandfather. When the children are besieged by the fear of Maggy's removal, just as they were besieged by the ice storm that strikes their house, L'Engle has them see order and beauty and appreciate the mystery in the unknown. Looking out at the ice-coated world, Vicky experiences something of an epiphany:

> It was so beautiful we couldn't speak, any of us. We just stood there and looked and looked. And suddenly I was so happy I felt as though my happiness were flying all about me, like sparkles of moonlight off the ice. And I wanted to hug everybody, and tell how much I loved everybody and how happy I was, but it seemed as though I were under a spell, as though I couldn't move or speak, and I just stood there, with joys streaming out of me, until mother and Daddy sent us up to bed.
>
> And I lay there in the dark and I was absolutely positive that God would not allow Maggy to be thrown to the lions. (*Austins,* 131–132)

Here, as in other places in the narrative, the beauty of nature exercises a power that gives succor in the face of pain. This comfort, as the following passage indicates, is something that L'Engle and her family drew on during the actual events that serve as the basis for this novel:

> During that same decade of the fifties we experienced a good deal of personal tragedy. Four of our closest friends died, and because we live in a small community our friends and neighbors were there with help and support. And the children of the village were not left out of what was going on. We talked about it with them. Whenever anything happened that was beyond the ordinary daily joys and sufferings, I would take my children and go to the top of the neighboring Mohawk Mountain to watch the stars come out, and to talk about whatever it was that was hurting us, and to try to make some sense out of it. We didn't pretend that bad things had not happened; conversely, we didn't project visions of bad things that had not yet happened. My children helped me to understand the need to live where we are in the immediate moment.[3]

For Vicky in the fictional situation as for her author in the real situation, nature provides a comfort. During the epiphany noted above, the goodness of creation shines forth so that, as Vicky says, "for the moment the beauty was all that mattered; it wasn't important that there were things that we would never understand" (*Austins,* 38).

The selflessness that Vicky feels when gazing at the stars or sea or the glaze of the ice storm is akin to the selflessness professed by Grandfather Eaton, a minor but thematically significant character in this novel. If it were not for his inclusion, the succor that nature provides might seem to be just a romantic nourishment of the soul. But because L'Engle has established selfishness as the root of Vicky's earlier problems, and because of Grandfather's clear articulation of his vision, the succor that nature holds seems to be a Christian succor. For him, the things of the world point toward God if they are viewed with honest vision, and his motto, painted on the wall of his house, is from a poem by Thomas Browne, a poem that, according to Vicky, the Austins all love:

> If thou could'st empty all thyself of self,
>   Like to a shell dishabited,
> Then might He find thee on the ocean shelf,
>   And say, "This is not dead,"
>   And fill thee with Himself instead. (*Austins,* 155)

As the poem continues, it becomes clear that the human problem is one of being too "replete" with self so that God says "there is no room for Me" (*Austins,* 155).

The hope that the novel offers, then, is the hope of a creator who filled the natural world with his love by shaping a world that is beautiful and orderly, hope that is necessarily built on the faith of things not seen. By showing us Vicky's struggle with the appearances of evil in the world, L'Engle shows a 12-year-old's vision of a fallen world, but by showing us her visions of beauty and her lessons in selflessness, L'Engle offers us a realistic portrait of a child's growing faith, a faith that as yet is firmly rooted in familial relationships and in her imitation of family members' beliefs, but a faith that promises to grow as she does.

The Moon by Night

Vicky does not forget the lessons of creation; she continues to go to look at the horizon of land and sea because as you see it, "stretching away to eternity ... you couldn't stay afraid because fears were so small they just lost themselves" (*Moon*, 67). As she faces the crises of adolescence, however, she does not find family as much of a haven, but comes more and more in tension with them and their values as she seeks to discover her own values and sense of identity. She learns much about the world beyond Thornhill, which, for her, of course, means the world beyond the safety of her family and beliefs, the world of evil.

The novel is a bildungsroman, for in it Vicky moves from a state of adolescent confusion to a secure understanding of her identity. While at the end of *Meet the Austins* she has come to a kind of resolution about the problem of evil, that resolution is based on her family's values and is set really in the context of her family. Now when she is a few years older that resolution is not quite as comforting, for her relationship with her family has been altered by her adolescence. In *Moon by Night,* she has to face the questions anew. The difficulty she faces is that the very thing that gives her confidence in her personal growth—her step away from the family—is the thing that most profoundly raises the problem of evil—that is, her relationship with Zachary, a young man that she meets on the family's cross-country trip. L'Engle structures the plot so that Vicky can formulate an identity that is not solely dependent on her family but is also one that is not solely dependent on the young man either. Whereas the conventional romance might require the protagonist to lose herself in her lover, L'Engle makes Vicky independent. Vicky discovers her own way of faith, a way that is built in the context of relationships but which is not dependent on them.

The change in Vicky's situation is evident from the first page of the novel, for what was comforting there is no longer comforting here. As she sits on the shore near her grandfather's house, she finds some solace in the ocean, but not the complete peace that she found earlier when she and John "stood there, not talking to each other, but feeling very close and somehow separate at the same time, because the sky and ocean were so vast and [they] were so small (*Austins,* 153)." It brought her closer to John—they intimately held hands in a way they rarely did. Now, however, she feels alienated from John, the family, and everything else. When she hears that John is looking for her, she resents him and the whole family for their happiness. She muses that because of her sense that nothing will ever again be the same, she is the only family member that is unhappy.

Vicky's problem is triggered by the move that the family is making from their home in the rural village of Thornhill to New York City, where Dr. Austin is going to spend a year doing research at Columbia University. But that move is only the catalyst for her reaction. The problem is more essentially an adolescent one, a problem of identity. Vicky explains that it is hard for a girl of 14, going on 15 to be satisfied with her age, because she feels like she really is not any age. She is "fascinated with boys," but knows "it isn't really time yet" (*Moon,* 28). She sees herself as an ugly duckling and wonders if she will ever become talented and get a sense of vocation like her siblings seem to have. Her self-awareness makes the issue particularly problematic for Vicky. She knows that this particular year of her life "is supposed to have been my moody year, my difficult year" (*Moon,* 8), but that knowledge does not make the experience of it any less real. She wants people to notice her moodiness and at the same time, she wants them to overlook it. She loves her family; she needs them for security, but yet she feels, as she later complains, as though her family is restraining her, keeping her from maturing and from developing her own identity.

In the midst of all Vicky's adolescent ambivalence, L'Engle introduces her to Zachary, a young man who, as a potential friend and lover, offers her a base of identity outside of the circle of the family, but a young man who also offers Vicky a very different view of the world from that provided by her family. A central question of the novel, then, becomes whether Vicky's attraction to Zachary will pull her from the philosophical sphere of the family or whether Vicky will be able to respond positively to him and his view of the world, accepting him but retaining her own view of the world. The issue, really, is one of faith. The plot positions Vicky so that she must decide just what she believes in—the God and system of belief that her parents passed on to her or the cynical hedonism of Zachary.

Vicky's initial reaction to his cynicism is fear. When she first meets Zachary on the family's cross-country camping trip, he sings her a song that in its black humor scares her "stiff." The song, ironically titled "The Merry Minuet," notes the atom bomb as the crowning achievement of human culture and suggests that the universal human emotion is hatred, a vision of reality that is exactly opposite that which Vicky garnered in the relatively sheltered community of Thornhill. L'Engle makes the song Zachary's trademark; because he hums, sings, or whistles snatches of the song incessantly, his cynicism echoes throughout the novel as well repeatedly unsettling Vicky. Like Zachary, Vicky is worried about war, but this song and Zachary's attitude shocks her.

Yet if she is repulsed by his ideas, she is somewhat attracted to his worldliness. Even before she met Zachary, Vicky had trouble understanding God. When the close quarters of life in a tent forces her to join the family in evening prayers, she confesses that at home she had quit praying at night "partly because [she] wasn't sure anyone was listening" (*Moon*, 28–29). In part, too, praying—particularly family prayers—seems childish to her, and she resents being compelled to attend church and Sunday school every week. It is not surprising then that Zachary infects her with his values. After meeting him, she finds the prayers even more embarrassing. She still participates but cautiously, keeping her voice low because, she confides, she could envision Zachary mocking her if he should hear her.

The experiences of the trip and of meeting Zachary force Vicky to think beyond the world of her childhood, to realize that Thornhill is not the whole world as it once was for her. As Vicky's attraction for him pulls her away from the security of her family and past, all of the problems of her adolescence merge with the problem of evil. She is thrilled that Zachary is trying to contact her at campgrounds all over the United States, but at the same time she feels so lonely that she wants to cry. It is a feeling that she does not remember having back when she "was a kid in Thornhill," and she believes that its cause lies in the fact that she has a new awareness of the violence and complexity of the world, an awareness that she has gained through Zachary (*Moon,* 71). She "was a kid in Thornhill" just a week or two before, of course, but what has happened is that in the changes and experiences of that brief time, she has taken a step toward maturity.

That step is not an easy one for Vicky to take, for it is a step that drops her from the well-lighted, secure world of her family into the dark abyss of twentieth-century nihilism. In his knowledge of evil, Zachary is a kind of demonic figure, in his own words "as old as Methuselah" and "old beyond my time" (*Moon,* 51), and he tries to get Vicky to share his vision of the nothingness. Death will bring "no pie in the sky" but no "burning in hell fires either." All it promises in his vision is "just nice, quiet, nothing" (*Moon,* 136). As he asks Vicky again and again what there is worth living for, she feels, as here at a campground soda counter, the influence of his dark vision:

> I felt as though I were being drawn down into a dark, deep, hole. The sunlight was outside. It was shadowy at the counter, and the blades of the fans whirring around seemed to suck me deeper and deeper into the hole. I wanted to leave Zachary and run out into the blazing sunlight, run pelting down the dusty path to our campsite, to get hot and sweaty from the bright heat of the day, to be part of light and joy again. (*Moon,* 96)

The tension between light and dark is really the tension between two worldviews—the Christian one of her family and the nihilistic one of Zachary.

L'Engle renders this tension more complex by using the play *The Diary of Anne Frank* to force Vicky to comprehend the power of Zachary's position. When Zachary takes Vicky to a performance of the play during a visit in California, Vicky identifies strongly with Anne. Like Anne, she keeps getting into trouble with her family, and like Anne she is halfway between the world of the child and the world of the adult. That identification makes the play all the more devastating for Vicky. Like Vicky and the Austins, the Franks use Psalm 121 as an expression of their faith in God's protection. But, as Vicky observes, "the Lord *didn't* preserve them from evil. He *must* have slumbered and slept" (*Moon,* 135). The realization staggers her so that she is compelled to consider seriously Zachary's existential question: "What's the point of believing in God when nothing makes any sense?" (*Moon,* 136).

The play and Zachary's challenge position Vicky so that she is at least temporarily outside the sphere of her family and face to face with the problem of evil. The position is not an easy one for her; Zachary was right when he predicted that life was going to be hellish for her when she steps away from her family's protection. L'Engle, however, does not choose to abandon Vicky to hell, for her answer to the problem of evil is not Zachary's answer. Instead, she uses Vicky's favorite uncle, Douglas, with whom the family is staying, to rebut Zachary's nihilistic response to the brokenness of the world.

L'Engle structures the conversation between uncle and niece in a way that suggests that Douglas's answers are her answers as well. He tells Vicky first of all that it is all right for her to be angry with God; indeed, that "the greatest sin against God is indifference" (*Moon,* 142). But, he suggests in a number of instances, our experience of evil is the result of our own actions, the result of God's gift of freedom of choice to humanity, just as Vicky's bicycle accident and subsequent suffering in *Meet the Austins* was the consequence of her "freedom of choice to do something [she] knew perfectly well [she] oughtn't do" (*Moon,* 143). But when Vicky protests that suffering like Anne Frank's still is not fair, Douglas submits that the nature of God precludes our understanding of his actions. Though it may be a difficult fact to face, Douglas explains to Vicky, God is infinite and is, consequently, impossible for finite humans to comprehend. Though there are "a lot of arguments *against*" the existence of God, the only meaningful response to those arguments and to the problem of evil is a response of faith—faith in a mysterious God, for according to Douglas and according to L'Engle, "there isn't any point to life without him. Without him we're just a skin disease on the face of the earth" (*Moon,* 144).

The difference between Zachary's position and Douglas's is essentially one of perspective. Zachary looks at human suffering and sees no hope. Douglas looks at the pattern of human experience and sees God working—sees a basis for hope. He uses the analogy of a jigsaw puzzle to make his point to Vicky:

> We jump to conclusions and decide that the one little piece we have in our hand is all there is and that it doesn't make sense. We find it almost impossible to *think* about infinity, much less comprehend it. But life only makes sense if you see it in infinite terms. If the one piece of the puzzle that is this life were all, then everything would be horrible and unfair and I wouldn't want much to do with God, either. But there are all the other pieces, too, the pieces that make up the whole picture. (*Moon,* 145)

In the structure of the narrative, Douglas's comments carry significant weight because throughout he has been the one adult who truly understands Vicky. L'Engle adds even more authority to his views by making this very conversation an example of how the puzzle analogy would work. While the two have been conversing, Douglas, who is an artist, has been sketching Vicky. The resultant piece turns out to be one of his best works. The picture represents a significant accomplishment for Douglas. Vicky's expression of her confusion has helped him to break "through to something [he's] been reaching for for weeks and was beginning to despair about" (*Moon,* 147). So what she and the reader discover is the complexity of God's will for humankind. Viewed in isolation, Vicky's suffering might appear unfair, but viewed as one piece of a larger puzzle of God's will, it can appear as a potential good.

Vicky may find Douglas's explanation comforting, but the views are still his views and not hers, at least not until she acts on them in the climactic scene of the novel. When she and Zachary have been trapped on a mountain by a landslide, she is forced to act. As they wait in the night, Zachary taunts Vicky, forcing her to choose between his vision and Douglas's vision. He challenges her to call out for God to help her, asserting, in his bitterness and insensitivity, that Vicky will have no better fortune than Anne Frank if she cries out with the words of Psalm 121. Zachary goads her until in anger she does recite the psalm, but to her dismay it does not seem to work as a magic charm. Despite the words of the psalm, Vicky complains that "the moon was smiting" them, "its light, cold and impersonal, was splashing" her "and the Lord was doing nothing about it" (*Moon,* 207).

But in expecting a charm, Vicky demonstrates that she had not learned Douglas's (and L'Engle's) lesson. In the events that follow her outburst of anger toward God, she does learn that lesson, for quietly and undramatically God does answer her plea. Zachary, in soft, gentle tones, declares to her his will to live, which is a renunciation of his nihilism. Though Vicky does not understand Zachary's change, she does recognize God's hand as well as the lesson in this. She recalls her uncle's statement that "we're always yelling, *Do it MY way, God, not YOUR way, MY way,*" and she identifies this as one of God's "peculiar" ways, for somehow, "the moon was no longer smiting [her]" (*Moon,* 208).

At the conclusion of the novel, Vicky has come full circle geographically, but she has moved in a new direction spiritually and emotionally. Once again, she sits gazing at the ocean from her grandfather's cove, but with an essential difference. Before, all the pieces of her identity were scattered. Now they have come together, and Vicky can express her identity and feel at peace about it: "I was myself," she says "I was Vicky Austin" (*Moon,* 218). That emotional maturity has come, in part, from the experiences and new relationships of the family's trip, but in the main it has come from her step toward spiritual maturity. Though she feels no more confident that she understands God or the problem of evil, she has taken a leap of faith, however small, and has seen God work.

The Young Unicorns

In the next novel in the series, L'Engle switches narrative strategies as if to raise the question of whether the Austin's values have any validity beyond the scope of their family. Where all the other Austin novels focus on Vicky or use her as a participant narrator, *The Young Unicorns* focuses on a new character, Josiah Davidson, and uses a non-participant narrator to give a broader view of the action. That action, too, takes a form different from the forms L'Engle has previously used. In a strategy that one reviewer suggests makes for "a more complete and resolved work than *A Wrinkle in Time,*"[4] she employs an adventure plot to put the family at the center of a battle between forces of good and evil, a battle that forces Josiah to make a decision similar to the one Vicky had to face in *The Moon by Night,* to decide between cynicism and faith. With its focus on gang wars and urban violence, the novel sounded a timely note when it appeared in 1968, causing critics to term it "frighteningly realistic and highly imaginative," a "great story that teen-agers will read with joy."[5]

As the novel begins, Josiah is stalked by his past. When three hoods in black jackets harass him, he longs to have his past leave him alone. Once a member of their gang—the Alphabats—Josiah is repulsed by the shame of his past association with them, just as he was repulsed by their violence when in the gang. Yet he seems unable to avoid contact with them. Neither can he avoid contact with members of the other "club" he had once hung out with—the church. Once a choirboy at the cathedral that dominates the New York neighborhood, he now just roams its grounds and chapels, attracted by the beauty and peace that it offers but yet distrusting it at the same time. Even his name dogs him. Bothered by what he terms "the indignity of being called Josiah," he prefers "Dave" to the name of the biblical king "who remained faithful even when his father and his sons and many of his people turned away and worshipped false gods" (*Unicorns,* 57).

Dave's problem, like that of the protagonists of the other novels in this series, is really the problem of evil. Neglected by his mother and abandoned by her death when he was six, he sees the evil and the brokenness of the world as the essential reality. His vision is not that of his namesake; his vision is one of distrust. His mother "was the first person to betray his trust" (*Unicorns,* 85), and he has never had anyone or anything to undo that betrayal. His alcoholic father, only occasionally sober enough to practice his skill as a cathedral craftsman, certainly offers no model of faithfulness or trust. Instead, as he surveys life in the urban landscape of New York City, Dave sees only evil. Crime and abuse abound. "You can't go around trusting people," he tells Vicky. "Not anybody. Not in New York City. Not today" (*Unicorns*, 53).

Dave's vision, of course, is largely correct. There is much that is evil in the world of this novel. Something is frightfully wrong in the city, and it seems to have something to do with Dave's old gang, who appear to be more organized than they ever were in the past. Even the Dean of the Cathedral is aware of the looming danger. "Over and over again as I walk the streets I get veiled warnings," he confides. "The Bats are preparing for something; the city's in danger; the Bats are going to take over" (*Unicorns,* 66–67). The Austins, too, get drawn into the trouble. On their way home from school, the children stop in an antique shop only to have an unsettling encounter with what they insist is a genie from a lamp. Moreover, the reader discovers that Dr. Austin is suspected in a burglary of the scientist who preceded him in his position, a burglary in which that scientist's daughter, Emily, who now stays with the Austins, was attacked and blinded. The mystery of the plot inheres in the question of just what *is* happening.

What is happening is a wildly improbable scheme in which the brother of the bishop—Henry Grandcourt, a talented but embittered actor—is impersonating the bishop, who—unknown to all—has died of a heart attack. The false bishop is using the Alphabats as runners and errand boys in his scheme to control the city. He is in collusion with a research associate of Dr. Austin's who is able to control the gang members by stimulating the pleasure centers of their brains with a small laser beam. Because Dr. Austin controls a few key formulas necessary for production of the laser devices, he and his family have been targeted by the bishop who seeks to use Dave as the means of getting information from them.

L'Engle uses this scheme as a typological representation of the spiritual battle taking place on earth. The bishop becomes a kind of Satan figure who, like Satan in John Milton's *Paradise Lost,* offers a parody of all that is good. His domain is in the netherworld—the subway tunnels beneath the city and the cathedral. There he reigns in state, "robed in scarlet and gold" with "cope and miter and jeweled gloves," sitting on a "chair, magnificently carved and mounted on a red-carpeted dais, so that it gave the effect of a throne" (*Unicorns,* 76). Moreover, in the light of the floodlights set up around the abandoned subway platform, the primate of the church looks "extraordinarily like a monkey" (*Unicorns,* 74). But most significantly, the redemption that he offers the city is in essence a kind of slavery. Through the use of his laser instrument, which in its addictive powers and effect on the gang is prophetic of crack cocaine, he offers security instead of freedom. "The only way," according to his satanic rhetoric, "we can be freed from the slavery of freedom is by relinquishing freedom . . . in a reasonable and pleasurable way" (*Unicorns,* 220). Such freedom clearly runs counter to the freedom that L'Engle favors.

But since evil here "declares itself as an angel of light" (*Unicorns,* 202), that perversity is not so easy for Dave to discern. The narrator tells us that "one thing he had shared in common with all the boys in the choir was complete admiration for their bishop" (*Unicorns,* 77); thus, when the bishop asserts that this underground world is not a dream but that "it is perhaps the only reality" (*Unicorns,* 79), Dave, though he is suspicious, is given to believe him and to do his bidding. And so he spies on the Austins and even goes so far as to help kidnap Rob, the youngest Austin. The bishop, after all, has been one of the few solid influences in his life, and as one character observes near the end of the narrative, "the tragedy is that Grandcourt was so nearly right" (243). Dave's difficulty in discernment, then, is not so surprising. If the Bishop is holding court underground, it is possible that Dr. Austin is also not what he seems.

But Dave's dysfunctional background makes trust and commitment particularly hard. He has been hurt so much that his one desire in life is "to make a great deal of money, to get even with 'them'" (*Unicorns,* 157). As L'Engle makes clear, however, his problem is that "he did not know who 'they' were. Were 'they' the Cathedral, who had opened doors for him and then left him on his own, to go through doors or not as he chose? Or were 'they' the Austins, who were so secure in each other that they could open the doors of their family wide for [him]"? (*Unicorns* 157–58). Dave fears losing his autonomy. He has responded to his past hurts by building a self-reliant identity, and so he feels that if he walks in the door that the Austins have opened to him—if he starts loving them—he'll lose his freedom. His choice to help the bishop comes as much, then from his inability to make a commitment as it does from his confusion of good and evil.

He fears the commitment not only for its own sake, but also because he fears the values of the family which, like Christian values, look foolish to the world. Unlike most people in New York, "they keep expecting people to be truthful and good," an expectation, that in Dave's eyes makes them "babes in the woods" and "sitting ducks" (*Unicorns,* 64). While they believe in an ordered universe, Dave is certain that there is no order. Where he refuses to trust, they believe that "people become trustworthy only by being trusted" (*Unicorns,* 144). Committing to the family would mean a commitment to faith, a risk that Dave is loath to take. His choice, as others have noted, "is whether or not he will risk becoming a part of something, a part of life, or whether he will continue to live alone and be part of nothing" (Rosenfeld, 106).

Yet L'Engle's theme is that such faith is worthwhile, for ultimately Dave discovers that he has to make a commitment and that the only commitment worth the risk is that on the side of life and love. He learns that he can not refuse to "take part in the huge cosmic struggle that is going on" (*Unicorns,* 155). L'Engle endorses his response by concluding the novel with a domestic scene that emphasizes his transformation from an embittered loner:

> Now Dave was able to look around the big table at all of them: Emily, who allowed herself to need him, and her father, who was not so lost in the past as he seemed; the two doctors, the Indian and Chinese, who had flown from Liverpool for Emily's sake; the two old men, so different except in their shared wisdom; the Dean, who could knock the chip off Dave's shoulder with the warmth of his laugh; the English Canon, who in so short a time had become a friend to them all; and the Austins: the Austins who talked too much, who were naïve, who in their innocence had freely offered him their love:
> His people.
> His family. (*Unicorns,* 244–45)

By committing to life, Dave becomes adopted into the family of the Austins, but into a larger family as well—those who have discovered the power of love over the brokenness of evil, who have come to see that "in a life in which there is no demand, there is no meaning" (*Unicorns,* 155). And by demonstrating that principle in Dave's life, L'Engle demonstrates the viability of the Austins's faith beyond their narrow world.

A Ring of Endless Light

Few adolescent novels face the problem of death with the directness and complexity of Madeleine L'Engle's *A Ring of Endless Light.* Though L'Engle had addressed the issue in her earlier novel *Meet the Austins,* here she turns to it again with an emphasis that suggests her degree of interest in the novel's theme, a theme that she says she hoped would be more directly articulated than it was in *A Swiftly Tilting Planet.* "People who can't understand the earlier book," she says, "may understand this one" (Forbes, "Allegorical," 18). The result is a narrative that functions elegiacally and, significantly, a narrative that avoids the pitfalls of many treatments of death in children's literature. The novel does not offer a utilitarian kind of "bibliotherapy,"[6] nor does it climb a pulpit to offer a "mediocre, soap operatic" sermon.[7] It does not reduce death to the "great fertilizer" (Abramson, 31), nor does it suggest that death is the happy doorway to pie in the sky by and by. Instead, it looks at death and the question of an afterlife frankly, developing a theme of spiritual transcendence even as it acknowledges the weightiness of death. The result is a book that, one critic notes, provides a "glimpse of the awesome, ungovernable mechanisms of life, and love that spans the arbitrary boundaries we have drawn between genus and species."[8] But even with its treatment of death, the novel, a Newbery Honor Book, is generally cited for its "magic" and the strength of its story.[9]

L'Engle uses death and the problem of evil to challenge the faith of her adolescent protagonist—Vicky Austin, who recognizes that her family traditionally has relied on their religious faith to deal with such problems as they face here. And, indeed, early on in the novel Vicky indicates that she would like to rely on the assurances of her family's beliefs. However, the exercise of such faith is not easy, for though she comprehends intellectually and, perhaps, intuitively, Vicky lacks the personal experience necessary to shape her response to the world upon that faith. A developmental theorist might say that she needed to move from a "synthetic-conventional faith" formed from "a synthesis of belief and value elements that are derived from one's significant others" to an "individuative-reflective faith" that might be "occasioned by a variety of experiences that make it necessary for persons to objectify, examine, and make critical choices about the defining elements of identity and faith and at the same time to critically reflect on those images."[10] In other words, until Vicky really lives with the ideas, until she acts out her acceptance of them in her relationships and until she uses them to face the despair that accompanies death, there is a sense in which she really does not own them. And it is that process of assimilation or acceptance that we see in the progression of the novel's episodes.

Though the novel is not merely a vehicle devised to present the issue of death, L'Engle structures the plot so that death surrounds the characters. The Austin family has come to the island to spend a last summer with their grandfather who is dying of cancer and who is not expected to live out the summer. Shortly after their arrival, they must face the death of a dear friend, Commander Rodney, who has a heart attack while saving a young man whose sailboat has capsized in the ocean. That young man, it turns out, is Zachary, who has followed the family to the island, only to succumb to despair. He, therefore, is attempting suicide when Commander Rodney saves him and, on top of this, Zachary has recently experienced the death of his mother. Every way that Vicky turns, she confronts some type of death. When she helps out at a marine biology research station, a newborn dolphin dies. During a visit to a hospital emergency room, a child convulses and dies in her arms. L'Engle even presents the move that the family is making from New York City back to a small town in terms of death. Vicky's grandfather tells her that leaving a place or a way of life is like experiencing a death.

The problem Vicky faces is what to do in the face of all this death. The strength of the novel is that it gives no pat answers; instead, it shows the confusion that Vicky, like any teenager—like any person, for that matter—feels when confronted with the problem of death. She sees that the people around her are living out different responses to death and realizes that in a sense she must choose among them, yet L'Engle does not make the choice that simple. The novel is more than a morality play. Vicky is in relationship with the various people with their various views and so must deal with her emotional responses to them as she sorts through their philosophical and psychological responses to death.

At the center of the plot is Vicky's dying grandfather. But his function goes beyond that of providing a catalyst to trigger the reactions of other characters; he is more than a death figure. Indeed, his centrality to the narrative has much more to do with his response to death. He is the patriarch of the family, and it is natural that the family looks to him as a model of how to respond to death. His model, though consistently serious, is yet joyful, based on his Christian faith. In the initial scene of the novel—Commander Rodney's funeral, at which he is presiding—we both learn of the grandfather's terminal illness and hear his affirmation of faith. As he comments on God's immortality and on human mortality, he makes a declaration of praise: "All of us go down to the dust; yet even at the grave we make our song: Alleluia, alleluia, alleluia" (*Ring*, 6). The grandfather's vision is realistic, one that looks straight in the face of death and yet one that hopes for an afterlife. The question of the novel is whether Vicky can come to assume a similar positive attitude toward death.

Because she is particularly close to her grandfather, Vicky listens carefully to his articulation of his vision and attempts to assimilate it. As he tries to console her and get her to envision the basis for his confidence, Vicky's grandfather reads her the opening lines of Henry Vaughan's "The World (I)," lines which provide the title for the novel: "I saw Eternity the other night,/Like a great ring of pure and endless light" (*Ring*, 64). Vicky learns that her grandfather not only is not dreading his death, he is anticipating, as the lines from another Vaughan poem, "The Night," indicate:

> There is in God, some say,
> A deep but dazzling darkness: as men here
> Say it is late and dusky, because they
>   See not all clear.
> O for that Night, where I in him
> Might live invisible and dim! (*Ring,* 64)

Excited by these lines, Vicky responds with a poem of her own, a rondel that repeats these lines: "A great ring of pure & endless light/Dazzles the darkness in my heart" (*Ring,* 66–67).

Aside from Vicky's grandfather, her family contributes little specific to her struggle with faith. Though she respects her family and although they provide a stable environment for her confrontation with death and the problem of evil, Vicky is striving to define herself as an individual, not as one of the Austins. Nonetheless, she does learn from her youngest brother Rob who, like her, has a particularly special relationship with their dying grandfather. Rob speculates that perhaps the afterlife offers something that humans do not have the capacity to comprehend, any more than sightless beings on another plant could comprehend a sighted afterlife, a speculation that one of L'Engle's children once made to her.

L'Engle's construction of Vicky as a typical teenager who is seeking to face her problems independently of her family makes Vicky's nonfamilial relationships thematically significant. L'Engle uses the romantic subplot, in particular, to dramatize Vicky's philosophical alternatives. The three young men who enter the plot as potential romantic interests—Zachary Grey, Leo Rodney, and Adam Eddington—present competing attitudes just as they present competing romantic alternatives. What makes Vicky's consideration of their views complex and realistic is that she cannot easily separate her assessment of their beliefs from her feelings for them as persons. She needs to try her views against theirs.

Early in the novel she thinks that Leo, the son of the deceased Commander, would be easy to dismiss on both counts—romantic and philosophical. He is short and dumpy with fair limp hair—hardly the handsome hero type. But worse than that he is pietistically religious. As she remembers him from the previous summer, Vicky recalls someone who "knew what God thought, and what he and everybody else ought to do on every occasion" (*Ring,* 31–32). Yet Vicky surprises herself by giving Leo a chance, and she learns something about pain and friendship in the process, but she only gives Leo that chance to spite Zachary. When Vicky goes for an oceanside walk with Leo, he begins to cry over the death of his father, and Vicky spontaneously hugs him and begins crying, too. L'Engle tells us that their crying is not only over this particular death but for all the reasons for grieving that inform the plot.

The incident moves Vicky along in her developmental process. The lesson she learns is one of the value of true intimacy. She discovers that her experience of empathy is more intimate than a sexual experience like kissing, and she declares, consequently, that she would "never again be able to think of Leo as nothing but a slob" (*Ring,* 33). The lesson, however, is not simple; L'Engle does not hold this incident up as an illustration of the ideal method of comforting a grieving friend. The incident introduces difficulties even as it solves others. Vicky is not able to think of Leo the same way again, but neither does she experience the degree of romantic attraction that Leo feels toward her. Shortly after this moment of closeness, Vicky feels ungracious toward Leo, perhaps, she speculates, because they had been more intimate than she is ready to be.

She is also surprised by Leo's behavior when he shakes his fist and eloquently swears at the sun. The anger indicates a new complexity in Leo's worldview, but even so, Vicky is not wooed by it. Leo has bounced from a blind faith to a desperate faith. He *needs* to believe that there is a God who is in control. Leo is no longer satisfied with pat answers about God; he is significantly troubled by the problem of evil. If God does not exist, he argues, "then nothing makes sense. It's all a dirty joke. If we get made with enough brains to ask questions, and then die with most of them unanswered, it's a cheat, the whole thing's a cheat. And what about all the people that die of starvation and poverty and filth—is that all there is for them forever?" (*Ring,* 227).

Zachary represents quite another attitude toward death, one that is essentially repulsive to Vicky. Still, she cannot simply reject him because of his views. Despite his apparent death wish, he and his family belong to a group called the Immortalists, who use cryonics to avoid death: his family has faith that genetic research will help to eliminate disease and aging and so they plan to freeze their bodies in the hope that they can be revived in the future. However, the thought of freezing a body to avoid death strikes Vicky as essentially wrong and as false as modern funeral practices. As she recalls Commander Rodney's body being lowered into the ground, Vicky thinks of that event as "more realistic" than Zachary's alternative. Her conclusion is L'Engle's message to the reader: "Being deep-frozen went along with plastic grass and plastic earth and trying to pretend that death really hadn't happened" (*Ring,* 44). L'Engle keeps that lesson, however, from seeming didactic by making Zachary someone that Vicky takes seriously. She disagrees with him, yet she feels attracted to and needed by him.

L'Engle makes Zachary both appealing and offensive, but, ultimately, less attractive than the third young man—Adam. Vicky recognizes that a large part of her attraction for Zachary is physical. She confesses, "Zachary fascinated me, like a cobra. And I didn't want just to be fascinated. I wanted more than that" (*Ring,* 192). Vicky finds that something more in Adam. She acknowledges that Adam does not share Zachary's good looks, but reveals that he has a quality within him that attracts her "like a moth to a candle" (*Ring,* 87). "Adam," she declares, "represented the adult world" (*Ring,* 191). He is more mature, more mysterious and complex than Vicky's other beaus, and so are his attitudes toward life and death. If her feelings toward Leo are somewhat fraternal and her feelings toward Zachary largely erotic, then her feelings toward Adam are agapic. Adam has a depth of perspective that both Leo and Zachary lack, and inasmuch as Vicky, or the reader who identifies with Vicky, follows the romantic attraction toward Adam, she moves toward a mature attitude toward death as well.

But L'Engle does not present Adam as a romantic and philosophical crutch for Vicky. Adam has had a prior experience with death that makes him hesitant to enter into new relationships. Vicky wants to befriend him but recognizes the difficulty of doing so because of what she terms his reticence. She notes that he is "alight and alive" when she wants to talk with him about his work with dolphins, but that there is something troubling that "light and life." At the funeral of Commander Rodney, Adam evidences a hurt that she believes goes beyond what he would feel for this one individual's death. Vicky's challenge, then, is to determine whether she can establish a romantic friendship with Adam, and whether, after discovering his hurt, she will be able to sustain her family's optimistic view of the afterlife.

What makes Vicky's task particularly difficult is Adam's fear of intimacy, which arises from his feelings of responsibility for a death of a friend Joshua the previous summer. Because of this emotional baggage, he attempts to distance himself from Vicky. As he summarizes those events, which also serve as the plot of L'Engle's *The Arm of the Starfish,* he confesses that he believed a beautiful girl that he never should have trusted and because of that Joshua was killed. Adam's hurt has also led him to repress serious thought of the afterlife. The events of this novel, however, have quickened those ideas again. He tells Vicky that he is once again pondering such spiritual questions because of his encounter with her and because of his work with the dolphins.

Adam's mention of the dolphins is significant for they truly do link Adam, Vicky, and her grandfather's vision of eternity. First of all, the dolphins possess a nonlinear sense of time that is akin to the grandfather's notion of eternal time. Vicky knows this because of her ability to communicate telepathically with Basil, Norberta, and Njord, the dolphins in Adam's experiment, an ability that "extrapolates the qualities of their natures just a discreet shade beyond what we are sure about."[11] When she asks them about time, her mind is flooded with a series of images, including a vision of the stars of the galaxies flying and dancing with butterfly wings, a vision that, as Vicky explains, "did something to my idea of time, so that I saw that it was quite different from the one-way road which was all I knew" (*Ring,* 269). This nonlinear time, as she sees it in her vision, is more like a tree with branches that cross and touch than it is like a road or a river—the same kind of eternal time that Vicky's grandfather experiences as he looks from his deathbed into eternity.

This link between the dolphin's world and Vicky's grandfather's faith is confirmed when Vicky telepathically asks Basil if the people who have died and who are dying are all right, ending finally with a basic philosophical question about the nature of reality, "Is it all right?" (*Ring*, 237). Basil's answer is to pull himself out of the water and to utter a series of singing sounds, sounds that the researchers had not heard from him before. His actions remind Vicky "of Grandfather standing by Commander Rodney's open grave and saying those terrible words and then crying out, full of joy, *Alleluia, alleluia, alleluia!*" (*Ring*, 237). In another instance, Norberta sends her a vision of a unified universe moving in a kind of cosmic dance, a dance similar to that of the farandolae in *Wind* and of the stars in *Many Waters* and other of L'Engle's novels. In fact, again and again in her communications with the dolphins, Vicky receives messages of joy, messages that affirm her faith, because "joy," she says, as "grandfather would remind me, joy is the infallible sign of the presence of God" (*Ring*, 271). Still, she cannot act on that faith, for immediately after her statement of epiphany, she says in what amounts to an aside, "But I couldn't tell Adam that. Not yet" (*Ring*, 271).

Before she can share this vision with Adam, Vicky has to face a harder test, perhaps because as she muses earlier, "Maybe you have to know the darkness before you can appreciate the light" (*Ring*, 218). Her test has two parts. First, she has to confront the cynicism of Zachary, and second, she has to face her own despair. When she is arguing with him about his apparent death wish and his willingness to risk other peoples' lives, Zachary accuses Vicky of inhabiting a dreamworld, and just as she did in *Moon*, she has to stand up to his negative vision. As Vicky meets his challenge by asserting that "the horrors aren't all the world," (*Ring*, 301) she can have little inclination as to how soon she will be confronted by what Zachary terms the real world. Within hours of this conversation, Vicky discovers that her grandfather is in a crisis at the hospital. She goes there only to have a young child convulse and die in her arms as she waits in the emergency room for news about her grandfather. L'Engle's intention is clearly to pose a trial for Vicky, just as in an earlier draft she has an airliner crash while Vicky is watching.[12]

The despair that follows poses the ultimate test for her faith, for she is no longer attempting to apply her beliefs to someone else's situation. Instead, she is facing her own darkness and despair. The emotional-spiritual state that she finds herself in is exactly the opposite of that of her grandfather. She recounts that she "was lost in a cloud of terror, with dim pictures transposing themselves one on top of the other, a falling plane, Binnie [the child who had died], Rob, Grandfather. . . . There was no light. The darkness was deep and there was no dazzle" (*Ring*, 310). Indeed, in her despair Vicky comes to believe that "maybe Zachary was right after all" (*Ring*, 310).

For a time it seems as if no one can break through to free Vicky from the darkness. Adam, who responded to her telepathic call for help, can say nothing that affects her. Like the biblical Job she has encountered great tragedy, and as Job's friends had accused him of being responsible for his own tragedy, her family accuses her of being responsible for her own despair. Her sister angrily reminds her that she has a roof over her head and people who love her, and her brother chides her for wallowing in her grief, telling her that she isn't "being asked to bear more than the ordinary burdens of life, the things that come to everybody sooner or later" (*Ring*, 316), but she cannot respond. Even Vicky's grandfather's reprimand and charge to her to be a lightbearer carries no weight. In showing Vicky's dark night of the soul, L'Engle accurately portrays the alienation that often accompanies an intimate encounter with death.

However, L'Engle does not leave Vicky in despair. Instead she completes the elegiac dimension of the novel by crafting a conclusion that is realistic but also moves Vicky (and the reader) to a position where she can see hope again. Vicky has asked herself why she should be "conscious in a world like this" (*Ring*, 321), and L'Engle effectively uses a stream-of-consciousness technique to capture her paralyzing depression. Yet L'Engle ultimately uses the dolphins, which because of their ties to her grandfather and to Adam, have become extremely important to Vicky, to liberate her and to connect the plot with the pattern of imagery of the title. In the hope that they can contact her when no one else can, Adam brings Vicky to the dolphins, and as the pod swims with her, Vicky senses that the dolphins are attempting to carry her from darkness to light. Even here, however, L'Engle does not permit a quick fix of Vicky's problem for, as Vicky relates, she cannot immediately escape the darkness because the light is too much for her to bear. It is not until the dolphins spank her and force her sputtering deep into the ocean in a kind of playful punishment and cleansing ritual that Vicky is freed—freed, significantly, to *play* with the pod.

The resolution of the novel imagistically suggests that the vision of the grandfather pervades nature. When Vicky is restored, she gives this account of the dolphin's behavior, an account that underscores Henry Vaughan's world view:

> The pod began to sing, the same alien alleluias I heard first from Basil, then from Norberta and Njord, and the sound wove into the sunlight and into the sparkles of the tiny wavelets and into the darkest depths of the sea.
>
> One last alleluia and they were gone, leaving Basil and Norberta to watch Njord and me play.
>
> And then they were gone, too, flashing out to sea, their great resilient pewter bodies spraying off dazzles of light, pure and endless light. (*Ring,* 323–324)

In her presentation of Vicky's vision, L'Engle shows a mature character, a Vicky who has grown through experience to test her own philosophy of life. For Vicky and for L'Engle, there is no easy answer to the horror of death, but there is a good answer. Having been tested, Vicky can exercise her faith in a God that would not desert his creation.

4. For Heaven's Sake

> I do want my protagonists to be perfect, defining perfect as thorough, thoroughly human, making mistakes, sometimes doing terrible things through wrong choices, but ultimately stretching themselves beyond their limitations.
>
> —"The Heroic in Literature and Living"

"Nothing that is worth anything is safe," L'Engle remarks, as she warns that "We live in a dangerous world, but we will never find safety in our fear." [1] That warning might well be the motto of the O'Keefe family that we meet in four of L'Engle's novels—*The Arm of the Starfish, Dragons in the Waters, A House Like a Lotus,* and *An Acceptable Time.* [2] The dangers that the characters face are various, from plots of international intrigue that place them in the center of conflicts between secret agents and mercenaries as in *Starfish* or *Dragons,* to unwanted lesbian advances as in *Lotus,* to the threat of human sacrifice in *Acceptable Time.* Yet in each instance, the dangers require the characters to make essential choices. The choices are generally between good and evil, but the options are by no means clear-cut; furthermore, the decisions typically entail risk. Whatever choices the protagonists make will bring serious consequences for themselves and may well endanger people that they care about. Yet they cannot shirk the decisions, for not to choose is, as we will see, the same as making a choice. Yet if it is true that in the world of the O'Keefes nothing worthwhile is safe, it is also true that the risk of commitment brings significant, if sometimes bittersweet, rewards.

Like the Murrys, the O'Keefes stand out as a more than ordinary family. The parents—Calvin and Meg Murry O'Keefe, the heroes of *Wrinkle*— are both accomplished scientists and sensitive parents. Calvin is a ground-breaking biologist and Meg, now "strikingly beautiful" (*Starfish,* 99), "could get a doctorate with both hands tied behind her back, but she just laughs and says she can't be bothered" (*Dragons,* 90). Their children are similarly gifted. Polyhymnia (she goes by *Poly* in *Starfish* and *Dragons,* but in *Lotus,* she indicates that she wants her nickname to be spelled *Polly*) is precocious in her knowledge of art history and biology, a gift that sometimes gets her in trouble with her siblings and with critics who are wary of "children who talk like adults."[3] Charles, like his namesake Charles Wallace Murry, is often silent, but his silence belies a similar thoughtfulness and masks an analogous giftedness in science as well as powers of extrasensory perception that, too, are akin to his uncle's. The other five children—Sandy, Dennys, Peggy, Johnny, and Mary (Rosy)—remain largely, if occasionally noisily, in the backgrounds of the novels.

The Arm of the Starfish

In writing about her art, L'Engle frequently talks about being "obedient" to story and about listening to her characters (*Walking,* 22; *Irrational,* 122). That certainly seems to have been the case in the composition of this book. L'Engle's original idea was to plot an adventure novel around the idea of scientific experiments on starfish. She was "fascinated by the strange fact that starfish and *homo sapiens* originally came from the same phylum" and that consequently "anything that we can learn about starfish is potentially important to our understanding of humankind."[4] Her fascination led her to enlist the help of a marine biologist to design theoretical experiments that replicated research that had already been done on the regeneration of tissue in starfish and other creatures. Her plan for the novel was to extrapolate from this established research, to have the novel ask, in effect, "yes, but what next?" ("Mysterious Appearance," 22). But as L'Engle worked, she kept being interrupted by new characters, characters that she had not included in her plan.

The first to impose himself on her was Canon Tallis, an Episcopal priest whose particular ministry seems to be the foiling of spies and the solving of mysteries. It was he, you will recall, who played a key role in foiling the phony bishop in *Unicorns*. But when he first appeared to L'Engle, he came, of course, with no such reputation. He came initially as a "faceless, weightless, colorless" figure, as an idea that L'Engle reports struck her as humorous because his name is an inversion of a baroque tune, the Tallis Canon, that L'Engle's family often sang or played on the piano ("Mysterious Appearance," 23). Yet the character of Canon Tallis did not really assume human proportions until he "walked, unexpected, into J.F.K. airport" in the early pages of *Starfish* "when Adam Eddington [the protagonist] was waiting to fly to Lisbon" (*Circle,* 93). As she described Tallis in that first entrance, she found herself surprised by doing what she rarely does—modeling a fictional character after a real person. The prototype, in this case, was Edward Nason West, canon (or cathedral priest) and sub-dean of the Cathedral Church of St. John in New York City, where L'Engle is the librarian. The modeling was, perhaps, something less than coincidental, for the Canon was counselor and confessor to L'Engle, "someone who in his own way" she says, helped her to "regenerate broken spiritual arms" ("Mysterious Appearance," 23; cf. *Circle,* 240–43).

The second surprise came a bit later in her composition of the narrative. She had gotten Adam from J.F.K. to Spain where he and Canon Tallis were rapidly embroiled in an adventure involving kidnapping and espionage. In the midst of this intrigue, L'Engle reports, "a character, Joshua, just turned up uninvited in the story."[5] When Adam wakes up in a hotel room both he and L'Engle are startled. L'Engle describes the experience this way: "My protagonist wakes up, and is very surprised to see Joshua just sitting there, looking at him—well, *I* was very surprised to see Joshua—there was no Joshua in my plot" (Soth, 12). As a writer, L'Engle was then confronted with the decision of what to do with this new character. As she explains, her "choice was then to say, 'Out! I won't have you—I don't want to throw out 150 pages and start all over again,' or to say 'Well, I guess you're meant.'" (Soth, 12). And while she, of course, resolves her dilemma by retaining Joshua, Adam has a rather more difficult time knowing what to make of both Canon Tallis and Joshua.

Despite their spontaneous entrances, or—indeed—perhaps because of those unplanned appearances, both characters figure prominently in the plot of the novel. Both figures appear enigmatic to Adam Eddington, the protagonist, and yet the events of the plot require him to decide whether or not they are trustworthy. Both characters belong to an unnamed organization that operates what seems to Adam to be an espionage network. That network is engaged in a power struggle with another unidentified organization that also is competing for Adam's trust. What makes Adam's decision particularly difficult is that he is completely unprepared for it. When he arrives at J.F.K. Airport, he is simply a young adult eager to enjoy his summer internship before beginning freshman classes at Berkeley.

The trip to Gaea, a fictional island off the coast of Portugal, to work as an assistant to the renowned biologist Calvin O'Keefe constitutes Adam's first significant time away from his parents, his first steps as an adult. To establish his lack of preparation for the kinds of pressure that he will later encounter, L'Engle takes pains to emphasize Adam's vacillation between feelings of immaturity and maturity. He views the airport phones and is tempted to call friends to impress them with his exotic internship, but when he walks over to the phones, he finds them all busy with people who, like him, were trapped in the airport by fog. The postponement of his flight unsettles Adam and he identifies, "to his own indignation and shame," with a crying child outside of one of the booths (*Starfish*, 4). However, just as he is reflecting on the fact that in the past he always had someone's hand to hold, he notices a girl about his age eyeing him. When Kali, that beautiful, rather sophisticated young woman, viewed admiringly by the other men in the area, singles him out for her attentions, Adam loses his desire to hold an adult's hand.

Adam's quick emotional shift is one of several strategies that L'Engle employs to prod readers to view the subsequent scenes with dramatic irony. It is much harder for us than it is for Adam to read the advances of this glamorous young woman as innocent. Whereas with the egocentric hormones of a typical 17-year-old male, he is "overwhelmingly proud" that she selected him, we readers would have to wonder just what she has up her flame-colored linen sleeves if L'Engle had not made her dress sleeveless so that Adam could be seduced by the touch of "the firm tan skin of her bare arm" (*Starfish*, 6). Her name, too, ought to give us pause. Are we not being invited to ponder when a character named after a Hindu goddess of disease, death, and destruction gazes with "limpid eyes" into the rather naive eyes of the protagonist? Certainly we have to doubt his assessment that "he was truly entering the adult world in which Kali already trod with beauty and assurance" (*Starfish*, 9). As he responds to Kali's pressure on his arm and as her voice, "fine as a silver thread," spins a web around him, he may be stepping into the adult world, but he is definitely not doing so in the controlled, glamorous way that he thinks he is (*Starfish*, 9). What we can see, but he can't, is that he is the mark of a *femme fatale*.

Adam's attraction to Kali is the force that complicates his decision about commitment to Tallis, Joshua, and the O'Keefes. Her overture to him at J.F.K. Airport is to warn him about the Canon, who is also waiting to fly to Spain, and about the O'Keefes, who she claims are enemies. Kali draws on her sexual powers, insinuating that she and Adam are a couple that share the same values, to manipulate him toward her perspective. "O'Keefe and Tallis are against us, Adam," she cautions (*Starfish*, 11). Her urgency and presence almost convince the young man, and he tells himself that "Kali, with her sophistication and beauty, did not need to invent stories to get attention" (*Starfish*, 11). But whatever particles of doubt Adam holds about her story waver when, to his surprise, she kisses him and says, "Believe me" (*Starfish*, 11).

Her warnings are enough to make Adam wary of the Canon later in the narrative, even after Tallis extricates Adam from a problem with Spanish customs officials. When the Canon asks Adam to accompany the 12-year-old Poly O'Keefe on the connecting flights to Gaea, Adam resists trusting the avuncular, teddy-bearish priest. Tallis declares that he trusts Adam as he hopes that Adam trusts him, but Adam's capacity for trust has been damaged by Kali and weakened by subsequent events: "But I don't trust you, Adam thought. Not after Kali. Not after you seemed to be in cahoots with a fink like the inspector. People you can trust simply aren't *in* with secret police kind of people" (*Starfish*, 28).

L'Engle uses the dramatic irony with which readers necessarily view Adam's decisions in order to develop suspense in the first half of the novel. This is particularly evident when the questions in Adam's mind lead him to trust Kali over Tallis and O'Keefe. After Poly is mysteriously kidnapped while under Adam's care, he is asked by O'Keefe to remain in his hotel room, not opening the door to anyone under any circumstances. Yet when Kali taps at the door in the middle of the night, he opts to trust her over O'Keefe, reasoning, somewhat sleepily, that if Kali were right, then O'Keefe was as tainted as Tallis was. But when Adam attempts to cloak his decision with the rationalization that rules were made for people and not the other way around, it is obvious that "his power of ratiocination is sabotaged by naivete" (Hood, 16).

The world that Adam steps into when he opens the door is the world of the opposing organization, a world, again, whose malignancy is readily apparent to readers, but not to Adam who is still prevented from seeing clearly by his attraction to Kali. L'Engle emphasizes his fascination by lingering over the details of Kali's appearance when the door opens. Adam draws in his breath at her beauty, and then notes the components of her beauty from head to toe—her shimmering hair in a tiara, her champagne-colored evening gown, her gold sandals. And Adam is apparently still mesmerized when during Kali's rather cynical briefing about the "warfare" that characterizes her view of the world, he cannot quite respond to her assertion that "we simply *cannot* let people matter to us or we won't get anywhere," an obvious indicator of the terrorist mentality of her father's organization (*Starfish,* 52). L'Engle's presentation of Typhon Cutter, the father, is meant as a similar indicator of malignancy. He is grotesque, spiderlike with a ponderous body and thin, steely limbs, and he is arrogant and rude, forcing Adam to stay awake and to talk about what he knows about O'Keefe's research. Moreover, Cutter's chauffeur and bodyguard, Molec, is named after a Middle Eastern deity most well known for its requirement of the sacrifice of children.

The decision facing Adam would not seem to be that formidable, but to him it is because he lacks the perspective of the reader. He has gone several nights without sleep. He has jumped from a mundane middle-class routine into the midst of international intrigue, and he has found himself the center of a fairly common young adult sexual fantasy—the passive recipient of the attentions of an aggressive, more experienced lover. Moreover, Typhon Cutter spins a patriotic line that seems at least plausible to Adam; like many of L'Engle's villains, Cutter has the devilish ability to use partial truths to cover his prevarications. Cutter suggests to Adam that the real issue is what this means—"what all of it means—to the United States" (*Starfish,* 59). That suggestion, it turns out, is true, as is Cutter's assertion that he has friends in the U.S. embassy, but neither claim is true in exactly the way that he means it. The issue *is* crucial to the interests of the United States, but Cutter is working against those interests, and he *does* have friends in the embassy, but those friends, like him, are engaging in espionage against the United States.

Behind all the intrigue stand O'Keefe's experiments with starfish. As she planned in her original plotting of the book, L'Engle has O'Keefe pushing the limits of what conventional science has done with the regeneration of tissue. All the intrigue of the novel is not built around the remarkable but scientifically mundane fact that starfish can grow replacement limbs. Instead, it is constructed around L'Engle's extrapolation from that fact.

L'Engle has O'Keefe working on the regeneration of tissue in large animals—dolphins and humans, tortoises and sharks. Such research, obviously, has significant social and, therefore, political value for whatever nation controls the data.

Yet L'Engle forces Adam to decide for one side or the other before he is aware of the range and significance of O'Keefe's scientific work, a strategy that makes commitment a central concern of the plot and that, consequently, institutes it as a crucial thematic focus of the novel. All of the major characters—Tallis, O'Keefe, Poly, Cutter, and Kali raise the issue of trust in one way or another, but it is Joshua Archer, the second character to surprise L'Engle, who serves as a primary catalyst for consideration of the issue. Joshua, who works for the embassy and who is an intimate of both Tallis and O'Keefe, mysteriously, at least from Adam's perspective, appears in his hotel room, and begins pressing Adam to decide to trust one side or the other. Adam's response to such pressure is to withdraw, to attempt to avoid commitment; he wants to think that "as long as he didn't commit himself he couldn't do anything too terribly wrong" (*Starfish,* 80). However, Joshua insists that a time will come when he will have to choose, and Adam, himself, realizes that commitment is an existential activity, that right and wrong often become clear in the process of making a commitment, a theme that was much admired by reviewers in the mid-1960s (cf. Light and Hood).

As Adam looks to Joshua for an example of commitment, he sees an existential model. Joshua has not chosen sides on the basis of patriotism or religious faith, though he acknowledges that the latter stimulated both Tallis and O'Keefe to choose the same side that he did. Joshua's motivation, however, arises from his love for humanity:

> I don't know about you, Adam, but I can't look forward to pie in the sky. I'm a heretic and a heathen, and I let myself depend too much on the human beings I love because—well, just because. I guess the real point is that I care about having a decent world, and if you care about having a decent world you have to take sides. You have to decide who, for you, are the good guys, and

who are the bad guys. So like the fool I am, I chose the difficult side, the unsafe side, the side that guarantees me not one thing besides danger and hard work. (*Starfish,* 82)

The distancing of meaning from traditional religious values, the stress on personal choice, the accent on danger and difficulty—all these are mainstays of an existential philosophy. Such an attitude toward life becomes both more concrete and more appealing to Adam when in the midst of piloting them through a storm in a small aircraft, Joshua breaks out into song, "bellowing the joyful last chorus from Beethoven's *Ninth Symphony*" in his pleasure at doing battle with the clouds (*Starfish,* 91).

But if his primary model is Joshua, Adam also discovers important things about trust and commitment from the O'Keefes. When he displays excitement over the starfish experiment, O'Keefe reminds him that exciting things often have hidden implications, a reminder that neutrality is impossible. But it is Polyhymnia who has the greatest impact on Adam, and unwittingly at that. L'Engle draws upon the romantic convention of the innocent but spiritually mature child to provide a model of correct behavior. Poly really stands at the moral center of the novel, a dramatic foil to Kali. Merely by acting intuitively, she embodies a life of trust that moves Adam to commitment as nothing else can. She loves people, including Adam, purely and simply, without guile (*Starfish,* 114). When he arrives on Gaea, feeling somewhat duplicitous and shameful for his inability to commit, Poly greets him with affectionate exuberance (*Starfish,* 99). Everything about her reminds Adam of trust: her voice when she sings, her actions when she shows him around the island. Moreover, as Adam comes to realize, unlike Kali, Poly trusts without demands for reciprocation, and it is finally that faithful trust that goads him into committing to O'Keefe's side of the conflict.

But Adam's struggle with commitment is only half the novel. L'Engle places his climactic decision midway through the narrative to emphasize the danger that comes with commitment. As O'Keefe reminds him when Adam takes the step, there is no promise of either certainty or security that comes with trust.

What Adam's commitment *does* give him is relief from the emotional turmoil he had been experiencing. What it does *not* provide is protection from the battle that he found himself in. If anything, that commitment intensifies the danger, for in the second half of the novel, Adam is required to act as a courier for O'Keefe, smuggling data while pretending to have placed his allegiance in Cutter's organization. That work as a double agent almost costs him his life, and, indeed, it costs Joshua his, when Joshua sacrifices himself to save Adam.

Joshua's sacrifice for Adam forces our consideration of him as a Christ figure, particularly in light of the names L'Engle has given to both characters. When, by allowing himself to be killed, a character that bears the Hebrew name of Jesus saves the life of a character that bears the name of the first man, the analogy is virtually impossible to ignore, leading critics to focus attention on "the Jesus-like Joshua" (Dagliesh, 45). Such an interpretation of these characters opens the possibility of an allegorical reading of the novel, thus suggesting that Adam's decision between Cutter and O'Keefe may be a type of decision between good and evil that is essential to the Christian worldview. O'Keefe, at one point, for example, tells Adam to "think of Joshua" because "you couldn't have anyone better to follow" (*Starfish,* 145). L'Engle asserts that her use of Joshua as a Christ figure was not deliberate, that she "could never *try* to write a Christ-figure," but that here as in all her writing, she is merely listening to what is sent by her muse (Soth, 13). However, her desire to avoid didactic writing may be behind her portrayal of Joshua as an agnostic; there's a nice irony in having a Christ figure who does not believe in God.

Whether or not his design as a Christ figure was intentional, Joshua represents a philosophy that, because of his function in the plot, lies at the heart of this novel. As he explains that philosophy to Adam, Joshua echoes Christ by saying that "it's the fall of the sparrow" that he "cares about" (*Starfish,* 82; cf. Luke 12). He wants to make the world better for innocents like Poly. Both Joshua and O'Keefe talk about making decisions on the side of life and for the future's sake, decisions that they recognize may have a high price because of the battle that is being waged against good. Their organization, in fact, uses as a password-phrase lines from Robert Frost's "Two Tramps in Mud Time," as if to remind themselves that actions on the side of life as they define it, actions performed for "Heaven and the future," necessarily have "mortal stakes" (*Starfish,* 145). But if they are willing to risk their lives in this conflict with evil, this philosophy also entails that they do not necessarily fight by normal rules of warfare. Insomuch as they might resort to violence, they do so only in self-defense, and they work hard at being compassionate but not soft-hearted to their enemies. When, for example, at the novel's conclusion, Kali is attacked by a shark, Adam fights to save her and O'Keefe agrees to try to treat her severed arm even though she was responsible for Joshua's death. Adam explains by saying that "even Kali would be a sparrow to Joshua" (*Starfish,* 242).

Earlier in the novel, Joshua had told Adam that it was not always easy to tell who the sparrows were, and there is a sense in which this is true. Yet to say so is not necessarily to agree with some critics that "the theme of the novel is that good and evil are not always easy to distinguish."[6] In fact, one weakness of *Starfish* is that good and evil are too clearly delineated. Adam does have a little confusion in the first half of the narrative, but the reader is never confused. Instead, the split is just a bit simplistic. The names of the evil characters all have negative connotations and physical characteristics to match—Kali and Molec, we have already mentioned, but *Typhon* sounds like *typhoon* and *Cutter* carries negative associations. Dr. Ball, the cleric who functions as a foil to Canon Tallis, pronounces his own name as *Baal,* the name of another malicious Middle Eastern deity. Moreover, O'Keefe's experiments demonstrate a rather curious sensitivity to morality. All of the experiments handled by an "evil" lab assistant become malignant; experiments on deliberately mutilated creatures similarly go awry, and even some "evil" creatures like sharks are unsusceptible to the kind of healing that occurs in good creatures like dolphins. A world in which good and evil were less obviously split would have provided a more powerful backdrop for this novel. Yet despite these flaws, *Starfish* is by and large a successful novel. As Ruth Hill Viguers noted in her review on the novel's first appearance, "the plot moves with such speed and variety, and emotions are so tautly stretched, that if there are weaknesses, the reader is much too occupied to be aware of them."[7]

Dragons in the Waters

In *Dragons in the Waters,* the O'Keefes again meet with danger and adventure, "enough," notes one reviewer, "to make Nancy Drew and her chums squirm."[8] There is murder and attempted murder, the puzzling theft of a painting, a kidnapping, a potential environmental catastrophe, and an attack by wild animal in the Venezuelan jungle. But here, too, as they did for Adam in *Starfish,* the O'Keefes provide support and stability for the novel's protagonist, Simon Bolivar Quentin Phair Renier who, like the O'Keefes, is traveling to Venezuela as a passenger on a freighter.

L'Engle plots *Dragons* as a complicated mystery, one so complicated, as a matter of fact, that even as they found it "plausible," reviewers expressed concern that the plot "might be confusing to less able readers" (BR, 406; Benjamin, 22). Yet if L'Engle draws on the conventions of the mystery genre to build suspense in her narrative, she departs slightly from the genre. Though the mystery builds from chapter one of the novel, no detective appears until quite near the end of the narrative when the Venezuelan commandant of police takes charge of the case. Until then, the young adult characters—Poly and Charles O'Keefe and, of course, Simon Renier—perform the sleuthing and try to sort out the mystery, a strategy that preserves the focus of the novel on young adult issues. Moreover, the shipboard setting limits the number of variables that the young detectives need to consider, thereby heightening the suspense.

As it was in *Starfish,* commitment is also an important theme here. That theme, however, enters the novel differently than it did in the earlier novel. Simon is not forced to choose sides in the way that Adam was. Instead, Simon must come to terms with a broken commitment, the breached promise of Quentin Phair—the ancestor that he idolizes—to the Quiztano Indians of Venezuela. As Simon confronts this broken commitment, he is forced to make a commitment of his own, one that involves choosing reality over fantasy and that, ironically, causes him to break with the past in order to connect with the past.

The past serves as a romantic focus for Simon. Like a typical 13-year-old, he needs ways to establish the uniqueness of his identity, but Simon has, perhaps, an even greater need because his parents have both died and because he has lived an isolated life with his great aunt in the backwoods of South Carolina. He finds his uniqueness in his identification with Quentin, about whom he frequently daydreams. In Simon's idealized vision, Quentin is a great hero who "gave up his youth for others" when he left England to go to South America "to help free the continent" (41). When he feels lonely, Simon attempts to feel "adventurous and brave" like his ancestor and hopes that "one day he, too, might be a hero" (53). It is easy to hear Simon's adoration when he explains to Poly and Charles that Quentin "fought with Bolivar, and became his good friend," and that, as a result, Bolivar gave the Phairs a portrait of himself that serves both as a focal point of Simon's fantasies and as the occasion for this voyage (41). Though an heirloom, the portrait was the last item of value possessed by Simon's Aunt Leonis, and she sells it to a supposed cousin, Forsyth Phair, who promises to place it in a museum in Venezuela.

The skeleton of this plot is based on events in L'Engle's own family. A century and a half earlier, one of L'Engle's ancestors, Miller Hallowes, left England to fight on the side of Simón Bolivar in South America and, out of friendship and esteem, Bolivar gave Hallowes a portrait of himself. After about 11 years, Hallowes returned to England to discover that his family had inherited property in what is now northern Florida and southern Georgia. Hallowes went to the New World, intending only to stay a short time, but, instead, he married a young woman there and stayed in America for the rest of his life. His cherished portrait of Bolivar, quite naturally, stayed with him and became a family heirloom, until L'Engle's Aunt Sally found herself in circumstances similar to those of Aunt Leonis. L'Engle's aunt fortuitously found a buyer willing to return the painting to the Venezuelan government, thus providing the catalyst that caused the original idea for the novel to crystalize in L'Engle's mind. She and her husband were traveling to Venezuela by freighter when they decided to visit the portrait in Caracas and the story began to take shape in L'Engle's mind.[9]

L'Engle's original idea was to portray a man and a boy who would sail together to present the portrait of an aging, yet noble Bolivar to the Venezuelan government. However, in the course of the voyage, the man would be murdered and the portrait stolen. Those elements, of course, stay in the novel, yet as she composed *Dragons,* L'Engle again discovered that the story began to change. As she chronicles that process of writing, she explains how the story, in her words, "takes over" and "the original story is forgotten" so that "the murder remains, but the portrait becomes one of Bolivar in his prime," and so that "a ninety-year-old woman appears" ("Books," 11). These changes mark the shift of the novel toward Simon. Both Bolivar and Quentin need to be young so that Simon can identify more easily with them, and Aunt Leonis needs to be in the plot to provide a link between the North and South American elements of the story.

L'Engle also revised the novel to emphasize the mystery and to establish a link between Simon and Leonis and the O'Keefes as early as possible. The first four of the five different drafts of the novel's beginning started the action with the ship under way, but the final version begins at the dock, a revision that helps establish a number of themes that L'Engle develops throughout the novel.[10] By starting with this departure scene, L'Engle is able to show the importance of Leonis to Simon's security and to invite readers to empathize with him in his vulnerability and alienation. Moreover, just as the scene offers a natural way to introduce the O'Keefes and several other characters, it also, because it allows them to mingle, permits L'Engle to situate the various characters on a moral continuum. Leonis, of course, rates positively on that line, but Forsyth Phair, by contrast, with his mysterious motives, already rates lower. The confusion of the scene also permits L'Engle to inaugurate the mystery with the attack of the first dragon of the novel—the forklift truck. The forklift incident locates the O'Keefes on the moral continuum as well. The 14-year-old Poly, of course, rates high and her willingness to risk her life for Simon provides a bond for their later friendship. Then, too, the incident affords L'Engle the occasion to reveal the special powers of perception that both Leonis and the 12-year-old Charles O'Keefe possess. Both of them somehow "know" that the attack of the forklift was no accident.

If L'Engle uses the forklift incident to create the kind of suspense that is crucial to the development of a mystery, she also intrigues readers with her presentation of Simon's curious guardian—Forsyth Phair. In one way or another, the elder Phair rankles or rattles most of the other passengers on the cruise. He quarrels with Inés Wordsworth, an attractive academic on sabbatical, over some sort of prior relationship, during which she threatens to kill him if he drags up the past. He accuses some unseen person of spying on the painting. He severely unsettles an elderly couple by suggesting that they wager a few pennies per point in a bridge game. The ship's captain recalls Forsyth Phair under a different name in a situation in which he ruined another captain's reputation. Phair is repugnant in Charles O'Keefe's "sense of smell"— his intuition. And, of course, Simon wonders just why his uncle insisted that Simon accompany him when the man does not seem to like young people.

While she has us wondering about Forsyth Phair, L'Engle sets out a large red herring—Dr. O'Keefe's mission to Venezuela. O'Keefe is going to the Lake of the Dragons, the site of a large offshore oil-drilling operation and the home of the Quiztano Indians, to test the effects of industrial pollutants on starfish and their ability to regenerate limbs. His concern—and the essence of the L'Engle's red herring—is that "there were rich and ruthless industrialists" who might do anything to hinder his investigation (*Starfish*, 105). That is why he hushes Poly when she is about to reveal his mission in a general conversation with the passengers early in the novel, and that is the source of his anxiety about Forsyth Phair seeming to know more about O'Keefe's scientific work than the average person ought to know.

L'Engle elevates the suspense in the first half of the novel through dramatic irony. By gradually revealing bits and pieces of the history of the Phairs, she exposes Forsyth Phair's real identity, so that we have a greater sense of Simon's danger than he does. We discover through Professor Wordsworth that Phair is really Fernando Propice, a callous smuggler and extortionist, and we comprehend what has been mysterious from the outset—the Venezuelan-American connection and the significance of the portrait. In a series of cinematic cuts, L'Engle takes us back and forth from the shipboard action to Pharaoh, the Phair plantation where we look over Leonis's shoulder as she reads a packet of Quentin Phair's letters. Though the letters were supposed to have been sealed for another generation, Leonis's intuition prompts her to examine them.

What she finds as she reads adds a crucial, if rather improbable, element to the plot. When Quentin Phair left Venezuela for England and ultimately America, he not only abandoned a country but he also deserted a common-law Quiztano wife, whom he apparently "forgot" in his attraction for his American love, Niniane. However, when, sometime after his marriage to Niniane, he sends to the Quiztanos for his portrait of Bolivar, he discovers that his Quiztano love, Unmara, died in giving birth to his son and that, although they sent the portrait, at least some of the Quiztano are angered enough by his desertion to curse him. The curse is that Quentin's sins will affect his children for seven generations, and the curse, apparently has been effective, for as Aunt Leonis mentally checks the family tree, she sees "the untimely death of a young man in every generation" (*Dragons*, 127). The question raised by the plot is whether Simon will be the next to fall victim to the sins of his forebears.

Indeed, Simon almost does become a casualty in an episode that L'Engle develops to address theological issues. In a suspenseful night scene in which a dark figure is stalking Simon as he strolls, lost in thought, near a railingless portion of the ship's deck, it cannot be accidental that even as that figure moves to push Simon into the ocean his thoughts are on the problem of evil and the providence of God. With a highly dramatic series of quick narrative shifts, L'Engle cuts between an omniscient perspective that reveals the menacing figure and a limited perspective that reveals Simon's thoughts. Filling Simon's mind is the memory of a conversation with his Aunt Leonis, a conversation in which she empathized with Simon in his anger over the death of his parents but in which she also expressed her belief in a God who "loves every atom of his creation" (*Dragons,* 116). Leonis's point is one that L'Engle makes frequently—that God "can cope with all our angers" (*Dragons,* 115), and that it is healthier for a person in Simon's position of bereavement to express his anger toward God than it is to internalize the anger and express bitterness toward the world. As he recalls Leonis's advice, Simon wishes that he, too, could believe as she does, but feels that somehow Leonis has been present with him as he walked the deck. What we know, however, because of L'Engle's narrative cuts is that he has indeed been protected from danger and death, a fact that suggests that L'Engle would have us believe that Leonis is correct, that there is a God protecting Simon.

With this episode and with the revelation of the curse on Quentin Phair, L'Engle has taken the mystery of the threat on Simon's life about as far as it can go, and she introduces the real crimes of the novel—the theft of the portrait and the murder of Forsyth Phair. These crimes present all the problems of a conventional mystery novel. They occur in an isolated community—on shipboard—and the list of suspects is therefore, necessarily, limited. Moreover, almost everyone on the ship could be a suspect. Motives abound. Professor Wordsworth had threatened Phair. The Smiths were clearly intimidated by him and had a skeleton in their closet that they were loath to have revealed. Moreover, a crew member, Jan, who is part Quiztano, behaves mysteriously when questioned about the crimes. The only element of the conventional mystery lacking is the professional detective, a deficiency that L'Engle rectifies by bringing the ship into harbor in Venezuela.

Once the ship is docked, three detectives enter the plot. Comandante Hurtado of Caracas fills the role of the standard detective of the mystery genre. He is suave, probing, and aloof, and his questioning of the suspects unveils all their secret motives. On the other hand, Police Chief Gutierrez of Port of Dragons fits the billing of the corrupt local official who, jealous of his superior, serves as a foil to the heroic detective. The third detective is familiar to the readers of *The Arm of the Starfish* and *The Young Unicorns*—Canon Tallis. However, Tallis, unaware of what he is getting into, is kidnapped by Gutierrez, who has also kidnapped Simon. Villain that he is, Gutierrez drops off Tallis and Simon at a remote jungle location in the hope that they will die.

Tallis is one of two characters in *Dragons* that do not quite fit organically in the plot. Tallis and the other "misfit," Emmanuele Theotocopoulos (known to the O'Keefes as Mr. Theo), are only tangentially connected to the plot. Both offer rather stiff set speeches on God and morality, themes that are more convincingly addressed by Leonis, since she does play an integral role in the events. Mr. Theo's primary function in the plot is to summon Tallis, something Calvin O'Keefe could have done as easily. Since Hurtado performs all the significant detective work, Tallis's main function is to aid Simon in the jungle, a plot problem that also could have been solved some other way. His only other purpose seems to be to demonstrate to Poly that all human beings—even he, whom she virtually deifies—are fallible. Both characters do, of course, appear in earlier novels, and their appearances here may simply signify L'Engle's habit of allowing characters lives of their own.

The jungle scenes with Tallis and Simon, however, do set the stage for the climax of the novel. L'Engle uses them to isolate Simon, thus positioning him for the realization that commitment is crucial to maturity. Tallis is wounded in fighting off a wild boar, and then when a jaguar seems about to attack their camp, Simon runs in panic into the jungle, an act that, in his mind, is equivalent to Quentin Phair's desertion of the Quiztano. Yet in this recognition, he takes a step toward maturity, for in recognizing his own failure, he is in a better position to understand Quentin's and to act to rectify both.

While Simon is lost in the jungle, L'Engle gathers all the other principal characters at the Quiztano village where she winds up a number of the loose ends of the plot. There we discover that "umar," the mysterious word on the back of the portrait, not only referred to Quentin's wife, but also served as the name of the seer of the Quiztano, the Umara. There, Simon is indeed the Fair One that the Quiztano had been expecting ever since Quentin's departure. There we see Aunt Leonis, who flew to Venezuela when Simon was kidnapped, peacefully awaiting death in a Quiztano hospice. There we hear about how Forsyth's smuggling operation with Gutierrez led to his own murder. And, there, too, we see Simon reject his romantic ideal of Quentin and accept responsibility for his own life.

Simon agrees to live with the Quiztano, a decision that L'Engle uses to critique modern civilization. When Hurtado objects to Simon's decision by retorting that he'll revert to savagery, Tallis corrects him by pointing out the savagery of civilization. Indeed, L'Engle shapes the entire presentation of the Quiztano to emphasize the advantages of their culture over Western culture. On a lake that is being destroyed by industrial waste, they live peacefully, organically in tune with the natural world. They can find people lost in the jungle when no Westerner can. Their medical practices are holistic and superior to Western procedures. Their attitude toward death is healthier than that of the Westerners; they do not fear it, but face it with grace and deep spirituality. Their culture truly is a place that Simon, who had been victimized by the dangers of the twentieth century, can call home. His choice to stay there to fulfill the legacy of his ancestor is perhaps a risky one, but that is precisely L'Engle's point: commitments that are worthwhile carry risk.

A House like a Lotus

If *Dragons* suggests the importance of making commitments that entail risk, *A House like a Lotus,* L'Engle's next novel in the O'Keefe series, examines what happens when such commitments are broken. In it, L'Engle develops the theme that was only hinted at in *Dragons,* when Canon Tallis failed to solve the mystery—the limitations of human character. Because no one person is perfect, commitment and trust will almost inevitably lead to hurt or betrayal at some time or other. That, Polly learns in *Lotus,* is a fact of life: "You won't grow up until you learn that all human beings betray each other and that we are going to be let down even by those we most trust. Especially by those we most trust" (*Lotus,* 82–83). But understanding that fact is not in itself evidence of maturity; rather, maturity, this novel suggests, depends on how you act on the basis of that understanding, on whether it leads you to cynicism or compassion.

L'Engle structures *Lotus* to raise exactly this problem for Polly O'Keefe. For the 190 pages, the reader knows that the 16-year-old Polly feels hurt and betrayed by her older friend and mentor, Max, but yet remains unaware of the precise nature of that betrayal. When, at that point, L'Engle reveals that Polly became hurt and confused when Max, a lesbian, made a pass at her, the focus of the novel shifts from the problem of betrayal to the issue of how Polly is going to deal with her feelings of betrayal. Polly is forced to consider whether or not she can forgive Max, a decision that is complicated by the fact that Max is terminally ill.

Part of Polly's problem is that she had idolized this Maxmiliana Horne, a wealthy artist and neighbor of the O'Keefes, who had encouraged her when Polly felt herself to be something of an outcast among her peers. The thematic pattern of the novel, then, is, in "three rather pompous words," as L'Engle herself put it in a speech, "idolatry, disaster, and redemption."[11]

Some critics have found fault with L'Engle's strategy to delay the revelation of the "disaster," because it "serves to distance the reader from Polly" or because "the premonition of Max's eventual action comes well before the description of the actual event."[12] But the strategy does two very important things for the narrative. Far from distancing readers from Polly, it draws us toward her, aiding us to see her in a more complex light, as a person who is trying to understand a confusing emotional event at the same time that she is struggling with all of the normal issues facing a young adult.

L'Engle's "characterization of both Max and Polly," as Roger Sutton notes, "is superbly delineated, showing the very human complications of love and friendship."[13] Moreover, the strategy allows L'Engle to treat homosexuality with greater sensitivity and complexity than she would have been able to if she had placed Max's pass at Polly at an earlier point in the narrative.

The development of Polly's character in the first section of the novel creates suspense that invites readers into the narrative. Indeed, when we first meet Polly, *in medias res,* writing in her journal in Athens, we discover that she is accidentally alone and that she is disturbed not so much by that but by something that had happened to her before she flew to Greece, something that she has not confided to anyone. Within six pages, Polly reveals that that something has to do both with Max and with champagne, too much champagne. That revelation in itself, coming as it does while Polly herself sips complimentary champagne, shows us a protagonist who is more worldly wise than L'Engle's other protagonists, a discovery that L'Engle made as she composed the novel. She wrote two drafts of the novel with Vicky Austin as the protagonist before realizing that Polly fit the plot more precisely because of her dual qualities of "intellectual sophistication and total social naivete" ("Acceptance Speech," 31). The realization, however, led to three more complete revisions of *Lotus.*

Both of these qualities are evident as L'Engle cuts back and forth between Greece and Benne Seed Island, between the present and Polly's recollection of the past, and both help L'Engle raise issues important to a young adult audience. Because she is intellectually gifted, Polly demonstrates a vocabulary and cultural literacy that alienates her from her peers as well as, occasionally, from some critics of L'Engle. The kind of girl who can casually allude to lines of William Butler Yeats or John Donne, who can speak six languages, and who is given to rattling on about esoteric topics in biology, puts off her fellow high school students. It also puts off critics like David Rees, who terms Polly, "absurdly precocious" (Rees, 59). But while Polly may not offer most readers a character with whom they can identify intellectually, she does offer all readers a character with whom they can identify emotionally. Most young adults know the feeling of alienation or of being misunderstood because of real or imagined social infelicity, and so most can identify with Polly.

The basis for such identification is most clearly evident in the social competition between Polly and Kate. L'Engle uses the popular and attractive cousin who is staying with the O'Keefes as a foil to Polly's character. Kate does the right things to impress the school crowd. Kate has the right clothes and more of them. Kate gets the dates and can handle social mores like goodnight kisses unselfconsciously, while Polly is less experienced and more awkward. She is tall and skinny; in fact, she confesses that the reason she alters the spelling of her name is that "Poly tends to be pronounced as if it rhymes with pole," and she fears that her appearance will invite mockery (*Lotus,* 7–8). Before she meets Max, Polly routinely expects that Kate will get the best of her in any social situation. When, for example, the school is casting parts for a production of William Shakespeare's *As You Like It,* Polly's first instinct is to avoid trying out because she is certain that Kate will get the part that she wants. Kate, in typical condescension, suggests that Polly should try for one of the male roles in the play.

Polly *does* try out for a major role, however, and she gets it—in part, the narrative suggests, because Max has helped her see herself, and the teacher doing the casting, in a new light. This is but one of the many incidents in the first half of the novel that illustrate the complexity of Polly's relationship with Max. Max is not simply someone who hurt her; Max is someone who shows Polly the world in an entirely new light. Max treats Polly more like an adult than like a child, talking to her about art and ideas, inviting her to dinner and introducing her to champagne. Max becomes her mentor, encouraging Polly in her writing and bolstering her in her self image by painting her portrait. Max helps Polly to see the loneliness in an antagonistic teacher's behavior. Again and again, as we see through L'Engle's flashbacks, Max aids Polly in carving a new, more positive identity for herself, so that we find it plausible when Polly declares that "through Max's eyes I saw more than I'd ever seen before" (*Lotus,* 91). We also see what Polly does not, that, in her father's words, "Polly has Max confused with God" (*Lotus,* 91).

But if the long first section of the novel allows L'Engle to develop an in-depth relationship between Polly and Max, it also permits her to raise the issue of Max's homosexuality with complexity. Max, we discover with Polly, is in a committed, monogamous lesbian relationship with Ursula Heschel, a neurosurgeon who is also treating Max in her battle with a rare tropical disease. L'Engle's portrayal of their relationship has been criticized for being stereotypical. Despite her apparently broad-minded intentions, argues David Rees, L'Engle "falls into the cliche perpetuated by so many writers: you can have a homosexual character if you show that person as being morally weak and/or you let him/her die" (Rees, 60). Rees also faults L'Engle for the butchy characterization of Ursula. But to make such charges is to miss the weight of a narrative that works hard to explode stereotypes.

As she spends more and more time with Max and Ursula, Polly has to come to terms with their homosexuality. The issue first arises at the O'Keefe dinner table when the two characters who are, perhaps, the most sensitive to public opinion—Kate and Xan—stop the dinner conversation by asking Mr. and Mrs. O'Keefe whether they "think it's good for Polly to spend so much time with those dykes" (*Lotus,* 107). L'Engle has the O'Keefes quickly assert that individuals are more than their sex lives and that gossip about sexual behavior has no place at their dinner table. Nonetheless, Polly needs to deal psychologically with the gossip. She *is* concerned about what her peers think of her, and she has a young adult's natural curiosity about her own sexual identity. Max has to reassure Polly that she is not a lesbian. But whatever concerns that she might have about homosexuality, Polly realizes that the school talk about "dykes," "gays," "faggots," and "queers" just does not fit the reality of the two people she knows. And with her realization comes the reader's education.

These attempts to avoid stereotypical judgments of Max, coupled with Polly's veneration of the artist, have made Max's drunken pass at her difficult for Polly to comprehend. Ironically, the incident occurs right after Polly has told her father that she rather prefers the "complication" of Max's life-style over that of some of the "normal" townspeople with their "cocktail-partying, wife-swapping, promiscuous lives" (*Lotus,* 180), and it shatters the vision of Max that Polly had been developing. Although in an earlier draft the scene was much more physical, much closer to a rape, in the published version the scene is discreet to the point of obliqueness. A number of reviewers, in fact, have wondered if most readers will even understand what has happened (Sutton, 91; Black, 50). But in making it so subtle, L'Engle makes the event more of a manifestation of Max's hurt and fear than an expression of her sexuality. She has been drinking heavily to counteract the pain associated with her disease, and she divulges to Polly that she is overwhelmed with fear: "Afraid of the dark. Afraid of nothingness. Of being alone. Of not being" (*Lotus,* 186). In reaching for Polly, which is, in the final version, all that she does, Max is reaching for affirmation of her being. As soon as Max does, and as soon as Polly flees, Max realizes the inappropriateness of her own actions. In fact, her attempt to touch Polly causes her to equate herself with her father, whom she hates for being, in her words, "a lecherous old roué" who had done much to destroy her and her mother (*Lotus,* 125).

But whatever Max's intentions or regrets, the incident violates and alienates the girl that had become like a daughter to her, and one of the main questions of the novel is how that violation will affect Polly in her other relationships. L'Engle raises that by introducing Zachary Gray, the ultrarich, ultracynical boyfriend and nemesis of Vicky Austin. Polly meets Zachary in Greece while she is alone, and she is flattered by his attraction to her but somewhat put off by both his promiscuous attitude and his cynical philosophy of life. Quite early in their friendship Zachary asks Polly if she is a virgin, and he interprets her reticence to answer and her moodiness as indications that the hurt she was obviously feeling was the result of an earlier sexual liaison. That perception prompts moments of sensitivity in him, but those, by and large, function as part of his seduction strategy, because sex is never far from his mind. In the midst of a conversation about trust, for example, he tries to arouse her, whining when she pulls away that "If you gave in once, why not now, when you know things are really fizzing between us?" (*Lotus,* 125). Given this kind of attitude, most of his responses to Polly's explanations of her hurt sound rather glib, but that is L'Engle's intention: to make him something of an attractive villain, a representative of a world that is the opposite of the O'Keefes', a world where money matters, not people.

As a foil to Zachary, L'Engle offers Queron Renier—Renny—an intern at the hospital on Benne Seed Island. Whereas Zachary looks "sophisticated and exotic" to Polly, Renny seems "serious and nice looking in a completely unspectacular way" (*Lotus*, 50–51). And for the most part, his looks mirror his function in the narrative. Renny *is* serious. When he and Polly date they discuss the tropical diseases that he is specializing in during his current rotation of his medical residency. Like other important male characters in this series he's working on the side of life. He can connect intellectually with Polly in ways that no typical high school student could, and he becomes her ideal man. In fact, when she is in Greece, he appears in a dream to warn her about the dangers of dating Zachary. Yet if he is a serious medical student, he is not without passion. Again and again when the two friends kiss goodnight, he has to restrain himself so that the kisses do not go too far. Moreover, after she has run to him in confusion over the incident at Max's, he and Polly make love. The scene is tasteful and emotionally realistic. Polly's need to affirm her heterosexuality and to love and be loved is understandable; so is his tenderness and passion in the situation. Yet his lack of restraint raises a question about his maturity.

But whatever readers may think about Renny or about Zachary, L'Engle's point is that Polly grants them a complexity that, for most of the narrative, she is not willing to grant Max. Polly cannot let go of her pain, even though she is aware that her misery is self-destructive. Her Uncle Sandy observes that the Greeks believe that an ailing patient could not even begin to be healed "until all bitterness and self-pity and anger were gone" (*Lotus*, 178). Polly is aware of the sharp piece of ice in her heart; it pains her, but she cannot let go of it. For most of the novel, the lesson she takes from her experience with Max is that emotional commitment is not worth the risk.

But L'Engle uses Polly's experiences with a variety of characters at an international conference on Cyprus to move the protagonist past her self-pity to a mature understanding of emotional hurt and risk. Polly's work as a gofer at the conference is the reason for her visit to the Mediterranean, a trip that had been arranged by Max before the incident that severed their relationship. As she works with the writers, publishers, and storytellers—all people Polly greatly respects for their apparent peace and success—she discovers that most of these participants in the conference have experienced some great hurt in their lives. Frank Rowan, whom readers met as a young man in *Camilla,* lost his leg and his wife in an automobile crash. Virginia Bowen Porcher, one of Polly's favorite novelists, in essence lost her husband when he was institutionalized for insanity. Another participant watched impotently as her whole family died in an epidemic. What Polly also discovers is that despite the emotional knocks they have taken, each of these people still embraces life, still is willing to take emotional risks.

Yet though she can recognize that rationally, she cannot acknowledge it emotionally until L'Engle sets her up to make a mistake that is similar to the one Max made with her. When Polly meets a handsome young delegate named Omio Heno from Baki, an island north of Australia, she quickly becomes friends with him. Polly enjoys his stories about his culture, and, significantly, it is his culture that has produced a statue that functions symbolically in the novel. The statue is of a laughing Christ, produced by the Bakians when they first heard of Christ from missionaries and assumed, to the surprise of the missionaries, that any such god must be consumed with joyous laughter. For Polly, however, the statue represents the joy that she no longer has, for Max owned a reproduction of the piece, and it reminds Polly not of freedom and joy but of her hurt. Omio, however, consoles her when he sees this sadness, and the two of them enjoy relaxing together and swimming together in the ocean. Before long, Polly transfers the kind of affection that she felt for Renny to Omio, and her feelings only intensify when Omio saves her and Zachary after a kayaking accident brought on by Zachary's foolhardiness. But Polly's feelings are crushed when she discovers that Omio is happily married, that she had confused *agape* with *eros*, that she was trying to take a love that he could not give. That discovery positions her to forgive Max, an action that is crucial to the resolution of the plot and that figures largely in L'Engle's philosophy. Elsewhere, she repeats George MacDonald's assertion "that it may be infinitely worse to refuse to forgive than to murder, because the latter may be the impulse of a moment of heat, whereas lack of forgiveness is a cold and deliberate choice of the heart" (*Two-Part,* 89).

When Polly does forgive Max and places a long-distance telephone call to ask her forgiveness, she experiences complete healing. As she does, the cold spot leaves her heart, and she experiences a blossoming of love presented in the same imagery that L'Engle had previously used to characterize God. Earlier, Max had explained to Polly that because of the abuse she had suffered at the hand of her father, she had difficulty imagining God as a father figure. Instead, she says, she prefers to think of God as a lotus with all of Creation being unfolded in the opening petals. L'Engle repeats that imagery in the conclusion to suggest the degree to which Polly's act of forgiveness puts her in synch with the all that is right in the universe. She has learned the lesson that Max had read her from the Upanishads, that in the heart is "a little house shaped like a lotus" and that "there is as much within that little space within the heart as there is in the whole world outside" (*Lotus,* 182). She has learned to imitate Jesus who "was more forgiving to those who made mistakes in love than to those who judged each other harshly and were cold of heart" (*Lotus,* 298). She has learned that nothing worth anything is safe.

An Acceptable Time

Because of its focus on time travel, *An Acceptable Time* has been marketed by publishers as the last novel in L'Engle's "time quintet"; however, its characters and themes connect it more appropriately to the O'Keefe novels. Polly O'Keefe is once again at the center of a plot that is set on the farm of her grandparents—Kate and Alex Murry, whom readers first met as the parents in

Wrinkle. That plot moves Polly and Zachary Grey back and forth between the present and the past of 3,000 years ago, where they encounter a pair of exiled druids who have settled with the Native American People of the Wind, a tribe, no doubt, related to the people of the same name in *Swiftly*. The time travel places them in situations in which Polly has to risk her life to aid others. L'Engle presents these situations in such a way that Polly discovers a theme raised also by the other novels in this group, that "Life at best is a precarious business, and we are not told that difficult or painful things will not happen, just that it matters. It matters not just to us but to the entire universe" (*Acceptable*, 230).

Though the characters travel to what Gaudior in *Swiftly* calls a different *when,* they remain in the same *where,* in the close proximity of the starwatching rock and the Murry's farmhouse. The world to which they travel, though, differs considerably from twentieth-century New England. The starwatching rock is there, but otherwise the topography appears foreign: a lake fills the valley; snowcapped mountains stand on the horizon; the oaks of the forest are older, thicker. In the place of the Murry farmhouse looms a circle of stone chairs, a druidic holy spot not unlike Stonehenge. Not surprisingly, the cultural topography appears equally strange. The peoples of this earlier time revere snakes, worship a mother goddess, and sometimes engage in human sacrifice.

Before Polly enters into this strange world, she is already vulnerable. Indeed, her emotional neediness creates one part of the appeal of the novel to young adults. Still grieving over Max's death, which has occurred between the conclusion of *Lotus* and the beginning of *Acceptable,* Polly is sent away from Benne Seed Island, where so much of the locale would remind her of Max, to the Murry farm, where her scientific grandparents can offer her a much stronger education than Cowpertown High, her old school. But sending her away from the island also sends her away from the people she is closest to, and so, as much as she loves her grandparents, she feels a deep need for friendship. Consequently, she is happy to have the rather egocentric Zachary, who is doing an internship in a law firm in nearby Hartford, show up for a visit. Then, too, her first thought upon seeing Anaral, a girl from the past, is that she may be someone who can be the "real female friend her own age"[14] she's never had.

L'Engle carefully develops this desire of Polly's for friendship to raise the issue of the nature of love. But the theme extends beyond friendship or even romantic love; here, perhaps more clearly than in any of the other novels, L'Engle articulates a Christian doctrine of sacrificial love though, characteristically, she does so by ranging outside of Christian orthodoxy for the elements of her fiction. Though this strategy may not endear her to those Christian critics who in their suspicions of time travel, druids, and other fantastic elements accuse her of perpetuating some kind of New Age heresy, it does keep the novel from being a didactic tract.[15] Yet it is this tension between ideas and story that has most bothered reviewers. Roger Sutton has noted that while "L'Engle's brand of Christianity is skeptical and undogmatic . . . too much of the first half of the book is taken up with provocative—L'Engle is certainly a spirited thinker—but rather abstract conversation having too little to do with the events of the story." However, to say that "ideas overcome" all other elements of the fiction, as Christine Behrmann has, or as Sally Estes suggested that there is "more talk than demonstration" about "love, responsibility, and human relationships," is to miss what is, as Sutton has concluded, a "somewhat melodramatic . . . but very exciting story," a story that demonstrates the power of love and the importance of selfless action.[16]

At the center of the plot is the question of why this time travel is happening. None of the characters can quite figure it out. The druids are split on the subject. They agree on the fact that Polly must have come across the time threshold to help them, but they differ significantly in their notions of the form that help might take. Tav, the more impetuous of the two, interprets Polly's appearance just prior to the celebration of Samhaim as the goddess's—the Mother's—way of providing a sacrifice for the rites. Karralys, on the other hand, believes that Polly is destined to make an equally central, but less drastic contribution to their situation. He, like the Bishop Colubra, a friend of the Murrys' and the only twentieth-century adult figure to engage in time travel with the young adults, surmises that the purpose of the time travel involves the lives of all the parties for whom the time gate has opened.

Zachary, however, presumes the purpose involves his heart, which is afflicted with an apparently fatal degenerative condition. The People of the Wind have native healers that he hopes can help him. And, indeed, L'Engle reveals that the purpose does involve his heart but not in the way that he intends; she uses his physical heart condition as a metaphor for his spiritual need. That need becomes dramatically evident throughout the narrative in Zachary's various demonstrations of his self-centeredness. Even though he reminds both Polly and the reader that he is "a self-protective bastard" who can only think of his "own good" (*Acceptable*, 82), his subsequent exhibitions of selfishness are shocking. When, for example, Polly is trying to avoid the "time door" because she knows that the travel holds danger for her, he becomes "suddenly fierce" and forces her toward the threshold (*Acceptable*, 195). But that bit of manipulation appears petty in the light of his later actions. After Zachary realizes that the peaceful People of the Wind may not be able to heal him, he deserts them for the more violent People Across the Lake that he believes to have a greater healer. In association with this tribe that seems to share his attitude of narrow-minded self-interest, Zachary helps to kidnap Polly and acquiesces to their plan for her sacrifice.

Zachary and the People Across the Lake serve as foils to Polly and the People of the Wind, so that the values and beliefs of the more peaceful, less selfish group are endorsed by the weight of the narrative. Whatever their initial disagreements about the purpose of these mysterious events, the People of the Wind, in a pattern of response that is common throughout L'Engle's novels, ultimately accept mystery as part of their deity's plan for their existence. Though that plan may not be comprehensible in detail to them, they have faith in its benevolence. Controlling the various lines in the pattern of their existence and governing the mother goddess is the Presence—a loving god who created and who sustains their world. Consequently, the tribe's attitude toward life is one of gratitude. Like many Native American cultures they thank the animals that they kill for food for their gift of life. Even in the midst of difficult circumstances—drought, war, and unknown danger—they express their gratitude for every aspect of their lives. Perhaps because of their peaceful attitude, they are at harmony with nature in a way that the People Across the Lake are not. They can listen to the wind and the waters and the trees and hear the wisdom of the Presence. L'Engle further underscores their virtue by having them impart this gift of listening to Polly, a present that comforts her in her captivity, but, more important, signals values that she as an author deems important.

But the People of the Wind are, perhaps, too good to be true. One flaw of this novel is the degree to which L'Engle imbues the attractive characters with extraordinary attributes. She raises questions of plausibility, for example, by making Polly an Olympic-caliber swimmer. Moreover, she gives the People of the Wind's healers knowledge of the antibiotic powers of penicillin mold and an understanding of rheumatic fever. Her intention, no doubt, is to highlight the significant healing powers of native peoples— medical practices that frequently have been demeaned as primitive by Western culture. But in doing so she undercuts the credibility of her fictional world by contradicting an earlier incident in the plot. There, she has Anaral cut her finger, a cut that requires stitches and treatment by a twentieth-century physician. But certainly, a healing practice that includes the use of organic antibiotics and can psychically or spiritually heal heart disease and other ailments can also handle a lacerated finger.

As she did in *Dragons,* L'Engle here, too, uses the native culture to critique contemporary civilization. It is clear, for instance, that she admires the ecological ethic of Native Americans. But in addressing some of the more violent dimensions of both the Native American and the druidic cultures, L'Engle occasionally climbs up on a soapbox. "What else is the electric chair or lethal injection than human sacrifice," L'Engle has the Bishop wonder as he and Polly discuss the practice (*Acceptable,* 174). And when Polly contemplates the skulls on poles that adorn the camps of these stone age people, she thinks of the experiments of the holocaust and ponders whether twentieth-century people were any less savage.

L'Engle tries to get the reader to see that modern violence is equally horrifying to a "belief that the earth demanded blood" (*Acceptable*, 283).

L'Engle's purpose in pointing to the violence that spans the centuries is essentially a theological one. Such violence is the inevitable result of human action when it is untouched by love—God's love. The plot accentuates the differences in behavior and attitude between characters who grasp God's love and those who do not. Karralys, Anaral, Polly, the bishop, Dr. Louise, and the Murrys all acknowledge God whether they call him Christ or the Presence, and all behave unselfishly, sacrificially. Zachary and the People Across the Lake do not acknowledge God, and all behave selfishly, violently. In between are characters like Tav and Klep, characters that may not like violence and human sacrifice but yet embrace it because it is part of the accepted tradition of their culture. Significantly, both of these characters are so impressed by peaceful acts of personal sacrifice that they renounce violence and acknowledge the power of a loving God. L'Engle keeps the novel from being theologically didactic, however, by distinguishing between the spiritual attitudes of the various characters. Polly, for example, is much less certain of what she believes than the bishop is.

Nonetheless, Polly acts out what the bishop believes, and that action is what resolves the problem of the plot. After she has escaped from the People Across the Lake, Polly willingly returns even though she knows that she is in danger of being sacrificed. L'Engle portrays her action as an imitation of Christ's action, and it has a similar effect on the world of the novel. Polly wishes that she could forget Zachary, that he would go away and leave her alone. But she cannot. In part she cannot for the very reason that she resents him—the commitment of friendship, the fact, which he ignores, that friends care for and try to protect one another. But in part, too, she recognizes with the bishop that even though Zachary is not endearing, the people that Christ died for "weren't particularly endearing, either" (*Acceptable*, 238). She returns, then, to captivity as Christ came to earth, not out of necessity, but "for love." "Whatever we give, we have to *give out of love*,"

Dr. Louise instructs Polly, for that "is the nature of God" (*Acceptable,* 185–86).

Polly's deed has a wide-ranging effect. It puts an end to human sacrifice, because the villagers are so impressed with her selflessness. No longer will the tribes scream, "Blood! . . . Blood for the gods! Blood for the ground, blood for rain, blood for growth, blood for life!" (*Acceptable,* 321). It establishes a truce between the People of the Wind and the People Across the Lake. They agree to live in peace, to share food and information. But most significantly, it brings healing to Zachary, Polly, the bishop, and the native healers, who join together to touch Zachary with a healing that "was not merely physical" but which pours "though the core of Zachary himself" (*Acceptable,* 332). Zachary's spiritual and psychological healing is not instantaneous, however; rather, it is realistically presented. He learns that he needs to let go of his guilt and that he has to work to like himself. L'Engle does not make him a convert to the bishop's beliefs, but she does have him recognize that the pattern of love is always there for him to hold on to.

These results suggest that the answer to the plot's earlier question of why the time gate opened is more complex than any one character guessed that it would be. That complexity and its resultant mystery is important to the theme of the novel and to L'Engle's view of the world. When at the novel's close the bishop ponders whether the gate opened for Zachary's benefit, Karralys counters that it is impossible to know the exact reason for their experience: "What has happened here, in this time, may have some effect we do not know and cannot even suspect, here in my time, or perhaps in yours. Let us not try to understand the pattern, only rejoice in its beauty" (*Acceptable,* 335). Though the question is slightly different, the characters come up with a similar answer to that of the problem of evil raised in *Moon.* The purpose of any event is much more complex than it appears to the individuals involved in it, but the confidence that L'Engle and her characters hold is that behind the event *is* a pattern and that behind that pattern *is* a loving God. "We are too small to see the richness of the whole," she writes elsewhere, "but all of creation is pattern" (*Good,* 191–92).

It is that confidence in what Christians historically have termed God's Providence that empowers Polly and the other characters in this series of novels to take the risks that they do. The world in which they live is a spiritual battleground between forces of good and those of evil. As Bishop Colubra notes here, "the bright angels and the dark angels are fighting, and the earth is caught up in the battle" (*Acceptable,* 239). The conflict requires the characters to choose between right action and wrong action, and though the choice is not always clear and though it is usually risky, the characters know that there are spiritual powers supporting the cause of good. Polly, like the bishop, knows that in an echo of Psalm 69:13 she can pray to God "in an acceptable time" and that He, as He does here, will protect her with guardian angels. The icon of a guardian angel that Polly carries is more than a curious artifact with sentimental value; it is truly an icon of what she—and of what L'Engle—believes, for an icon, after all, "bears a fragment of reality" (*Circle,* 18).

5. Angels in the Desert

> There is a violent kind of truth, a timely truth, in the most prim-
> itive myths because probably the most important thing those
> first storytellers did for their listeners back in the dim past in
> their tales of gods and giants and fabulous beasts was to affirm
> that the gods are not irrational, that there is structure and
> meaning to the universe: God is responsible for his creation.
> Truth happens in these myths. That is why they have lasted.
> Had they not been expressions of truth they would have long ago
> been forgotten. One of the great historical pieces of evidence for
> this is the Bible, both the Old and New Testaments. Many books
> that were once in the Bible have dropped out of sight through
> the centuries. Those that have stayed with us are those that con-
> tain truth that speaks to us in our daily living, right where we
> are now.
>
> —"Before Babel"

One of L'Engle's interests throughout her career has been to
retell stories that appear in the Bible. She has done so in a number of genres. She works in poetry in *A Cry like a Bell;* she works
in drama in *Journey with Jonah;* she works in prose in *Ladder of
Angels* and *The Glorious Impossible.*[1] But it is in her fiction—in
Many Waters, Dance in the Desert, and *The Sphinx at Dawn*—
that she is most successful in her re-creations.[2] In these works

111

she uses her powers of narrative to flesh out stories that were told in the Bible and to speculate on what might have been. She offers her vision of what life was like for young adults in Noah's day, and she speculates on some of the crises that Jesus must have faced as he grew from infancy through his teen years and into adulthood. But uniting all the stories is the theme that stands at the heart of much of L'Engle's work—that God is a god of love and that such love cannot be quenched.

In *Many Waters,* we meet the Murrys again, but this time, L'Engle moves away from Meg's perspective and writes instead from that of the empirically minded twins, Sandy and Dennys, who were in the background of the novels about the Murrys and O'Keefes. Though this novel, like those in the time trilogy, deals with travel through time, and though it is sometimes marketed as the fourth work in a "time quartet," L'Engle's shift in narrative strategy makes it a very different kind of novel from those in the trilogy. Whereas in each of those L'Engle draws the reader into the narrative by dramatizing the psychological or spiritual quest of the protagonist, here L'Engle engages the reader by dramatizing the world in which the dual protagonists accidentally find themselves. If Meg and Charles Wallace were on quests, Sandy and Dennys are on an adventure. The focus of the narrative, then, is the alternate world and their response to it; "the characters," noted one reviewer, "are subservient to atmosphere, incident, and ideas."[3] Because L'Engle drops them into a world of myth, we are eager to see what they learn about that world and how that world compares to the twentieth-century world of their (and our) "reality." The comparison does raise questions about some twentieth-century practices like pollution and nuclear brinkmanship, but, as Susan Cooper points out, "no didactic conclusion is forced out of them."[4]

That world, however, is one that stretches their sense of reality. When the twins type the command "take me somewhere warm" on what, unbeknownst to them, is the keyboard of their father's time machine, they do not expect that they will end up on an oasis with Noah in pre-Flood Palestine. But L'Engle draws on her theological sense of a gradual Fall to make that experience even more difficult for the twins to accept. Because they are closer in time to the

Fall of Adam and Eve, they are closer to the ideal world of Eden. The world of Noah is one populated by manticores and griffins, by miniature mammoths and unicorns; it is a world in which humans live hundreds of years, in which everyone can still can see angels, and in which some can still converse intimately with God. Because, as the readers of the other Murry books know, the twins are the "normal" members of that somewhat eccentric family: they are the literalists who in the time trilogy doubted what could not be empirically proven. Their challenge is to discover both the imagination and faith to deal with events that are anything but ordinary according to their former sense of things. Moreover, L'Engle places them in situations that test their integrity. In their own world the twins' identities were intertwined; here each of the twins is required to make individual decisions, decisions that touch on matters of trust and responsibility.

Their sudden insertion into the desert threatens the twins' epistemology. Not only are they uncertain about their location and time, but they are immediately forced to examine the relationship in their minds between belief and knowledge. Though they are startled by the small stature of Japheth—the first human that they meet—and Higgaion—the first creature, a mammoth—that they meet, they can fairly easily rationalize this fact based on their knowledge of the evolutionary pattern of horses. But then L'Engle has Japheth throw them a philosophical curve by suggesting that they travel across the desert on unicorns. The twins quickly point out that "they've never gone in for mythical beasts" (*Waters,* 25). What is particularly problematic for the twins is the fact that the appearance of the unicorns is dependent on the humans' belief in their existence. Like virtual particles, unicorns "tend to be," but they still need to be called by a human that believes in them. When Sandy tries to explain the twins' perplexity to Japheth by saying that "unicorns have never been a matter of particular importance before" (*Waters,* 25), he is making a significant revelation about their characters. As Dennys notes earlier, the two of them have "never had very willing suspensions of disbelief" (*Waters,* 23). And even though they are by their own admission "the pragmatists of the family" (*Waters,* 23), they have difficulty exercising faith even when it will serve them. Although a unicorn could save his life, Sandy resists calling one late in the narrative, and, in fact, he does so only when he can convince himself that his seeing unicorns earlier constitutes empirical evidence of their existence. Pure belief does not come easy to them.

Decisions of any kind are rendered even more difficult by the fact that the twins become separated for the first time in their lives. Because of the severity of his sunburn, Dennys cannot sustain the consciousness that is required to keep his unicorn mount visible. Consequently, he fades out of reality with his unicorn only to be recalled at a different part of the oasis. Dennys ends up in Noah's tent, while Sandy arrives in that of Noah's father, Lamech. L'Engle uses the split to force the twins to come to terms with their emerging sexual identities. When Sandy is ministered to by one of Noah's daughters, the narrator announces that "for the first time in his life, Sandy had a flash of gratitude that Dennys was not with him" (*Waters*, 38). But even as he feels the first twinges of sexual jealousy, Sandy also experiences significant separation anxiety. This is the first time in his life that he has slept apart from his brother; even at camp, they had shared a cabin. Moreover, because of their objective natures and their social success, the twins have never been very self-reflective. "Their relationship," according to L'Engle, "isn't something they have ever articulated" because "they have never needed to articulate it" (Schmidt, 12). The question raised by the narrative is just how they will express their identities now that they need to.

The pre-Flood world, as L'Engle draws it, offers a clearly defined moral context for the twins' action. Good and evil are sharply bifurcated. The good human characters—Lamech, Noah, and their kin—still communicate with El, as do the angelic characters on the side of good—the seraphim. The good humans live orderly, faithful lives; the good angels serve as guardians and healers, voluntarily submissive to the authority of El. They have faith in the deity's providential care and are willing to live with mystery. On the other hand, the evil human characters—Tiglah and her family—scarcely communicate with each other, much less with El, and the angelic characters on the other side of good—the nephilim—are similarly out of communication with El. The evil humans live dirty, perfidious lives; the fallen angels promote self-ishness and sensuality, tempting humans to lives of hedonism.

Even the animals are divided into two camps. On the one hand are the miniature mammoths that aid in calling unicorns and serve the humans by scenting water, and on the other are the manticores that roam the desert seeking to devour whatever or whomever they can. L'Engle highlights this division through her classification of the animals associated with the two varieties of angels. Both seraphim and nephilim at times inhabit animal hosts, but L'Engle uses the type of host to further characterize the angelic beings. The seraphim inhabit creatures notable for their usefulness or their connotations of nobility or gentleness—a camel, a pelican, a lion, a golden bat, a golden snake, a giraffe, a snow leopard, a soft gray mouse. The nephilim occupy creatures notable for their viciousness or their connotations of ignobility—a vulture, a crocodile, a mosquito, a skink, a slug.

But if the moral atmosphere of the oasis is obvious to readers it is not so apparent to the twins. L'Engle heightens the suspense of the adventure through dramatic irony. While the twins recover from their sunstrokes, readers observe the nephilim successfully seduce Malah and attempt to seduce Yalith with a line that was first used in the Garden of Eden. "Oh, little one, little innocent one," says a nephil to Yalith, "how much you have to learn, about men's ways, and about El's ways, which are not men's ways. Will you let me teach you?" (*Waters,* 47). Even if readers did not over-hear the nephilim agree to tempt the twins with lust, they would recognize the wrongness of Tiglah's caresses and kisses. But though Sandy recognizes that he, perhaps, is not ready for Tiglah, he cannot resist accepting her flirtations.

But the real test of the twins' relationship comes out of their mutual attraction to Yalith. It is not really surprising that two av-erage American teenage boys would take special notice of a girl who "was gently curved with small rosy breasts," a girl "who wore only a loincloth" (*Waters,* 36). Dennys fantasizes about the "touch of her delicate fingers" (*Waters,* 161), and that Sandy rhapsodizes about her demonstrates his complete enamorment:

> Yalith was not silly or giggly and she did not show off and she
> was not at all like any of the girls at school. Even though he
> had been dizzy with fever that first night in Grandfather
> Lamech's tent, his memory of Yalith was a vivid as though she
> had come with the stone lamp the night before. Her bronze
> hair had held sunlight even in the dark shadows of the tent.
> Her body was tiny and perfect. Her eyes, like her hair, held
> sunlight. (*Waters,* 151)

But it is not simply her physical appearance that gets the boys' attention. When he compares her to Tiglah, Sandy makes an analysis that is similar to Vicky Austin's comparative assessment of Zachary Gray and Adam Eddington. Tiglah is gorgeous, but Yalith possesses an attribute that makes her more than gorgeous. In short, Yalith becomes the romantic ideal for both twins.

The temptation that Yalith represents is not as much lust as it is selfishness—the most basic enticement of the nephilim. When Sandy discovers that Yalith has also ministered to Dennys, he "was washed over with a sick wave of jealousy" (*Waters,* 151). When Dennys discovers he is to be reunited with his twin, he feels ambivalent because of his attraction to Yalith: because of his separation anxiety, he wants to see Sandy again, but at the same time, he is not at all eager to relinquish Yalith. After meeting her, the twins, who have always communicated with each other, become reticent. Moreover, though the seraphim urge on them the importance of not changing anything during their sojourn in the past, both Sandy and Dennys come individually to the conclusion that for Yalith they might be willing to alter history. The temptation is for them to harden their hearts, to imitate the very behavior that "repents El that he has made human creatures" (*Waters,* 105).

Their problem is rendered more complicated by the fact that in the little they recall of Biblical narrative Yalith is not mentioned. Thus in facing their feelings toward Yalith, they also have to face the possibility that God may destroy her along with the rest of the population. In essence, they have to confront the problem of evil. As the twins discuss the Flood, they are baffled by the situation. They cannot understand how God could be behind this flood. Although throughout the narrative the twins have grown to a deeper understanding of God by watching Lamech and Noah obediently serve him, here they are tempted to turn away from him because of his apparent disregard for the young woman they love.

Yalith, herself, however, offers the answer to their problem—faith. She tells the twins what the stars have told her—"fear not" (*Waters*, 275; 282). When Sandy and Dennys rationally insist that either the stars or her father must be wrong, Yalith counters that she trusts her father and the stars. Her statement is an expression of a theme that is crucial to an understanding of the novel—that God created and now sustains the universe in love. Like the Elizabethan music of the spheres, the song of the stars that Yalith hears is a song of love. It is a song that on one occasion Dennys also hears. Sitting alone on what is perhaps the Near Eastern equivalent of the Murry's star-watching rock, he listens to the stars and imagines the violence of Creation, but he also hears something more:

> The song of the wind softened, gentled. Behind the violence of the birthing of galaxies and stars and planets came a quiet and tender melody, a gentle love song. All the raging of creation, the continuing hydrogen explosions on the countless suns, the heaving of planetary bodies, all was enfolded in a patient waiting love. (*Waters*, 280)

What the stars say, what the seraphim know, what Yalith hears, is this: *"Do not seek to comprehend. All shall be well. Wait. Patience. Wait. You do not always have to do something. Wait."* (*Waters*, 281).

This trust is what is required of Noah as well. When God instructs him to build an ark he is baffled and upset. "El has asked me to do strange things," he says. "I do not understand" (*Waters*, 210). L'Engle develops this thread of the plot to emphasize the sometimes irrational nature of things that require faith. The strangeness of the command leads Noah's family to question the sanity of Noah and of God. Ham and his wife Elisheba query Noah as to whether he really heard the Voice of El or whether he could have heard the clever mimicry of a nephil. Even the more devout Japheth and Oholibamah wonder at the command, though when

Japheth comments that the command does not "sound like El," Oholibamah retorts that "We do not know what El does or does not sound like. El is a great mystery" (*Waters,* 220). The only appropriate response to a deity who is both sovereign and mysterious is obedience. Noah's reply to the question of how he is going to face everyone when he builds this ark and nothing happens is simple: "I obey El" (*Waters,* 249).

But even with their obedience, the problem of Yalith remains. The twins find it difficult to do what the stars have advised—to trust and wait. Sandy concocts a plan to carry Yalith with them to the twentieth century, a plan that Yalith and Oholibamah recognize as wrong because of its betrayal of faith, a plan that Dennys identifies as impractical because of Yalith's lack of immunities. Yet Yalith would not be a plausible character if she were not troubled by what she faces. "I wish," she whispers, "that Grandfather Lamech was still alive. I wish that El had not told my father to build an ark, or that the rains were going to come" (*Waters,* 289). Yet her fear does not shake her faith, and as she is comforted in this moment of doubt by her sister, L'Engle uses the backdrop of nature as a symbol of the joy that upholds the Creation. As the sunrise flushes the sky with color, "A burst of joyous birdsong filled the air around them, and the baboons began to clap their hands" (*Waters,* 290).

At this point in the narrative, Yalith becomes the author's problem. What *can* be done with her? To put her on the ark alters the biblical source of the fiction. To let her drown runs counter to the impetus of the plot—authors do not generally kill off sympathetic characters. Moreover, drowning her undercuts the theme that love sustains the Creation. L'Engle eschews each of these alternatives to develop an option based on the example of another biblical character—Lamech's grandfather, Enoch, who "walked with God." Perhaps in part L'Engle saves Yalith *deus ex machina* to assert that women as well as men can be so holy and so blessed by God, but certainly she exercises this option to underscore the theme that "many waters cannot quench love" (*Waters,* 296). The love that Yalith holds for the twins is pure, undefiled by lust; it is analogous to the love that God has for his people. And so as the seraphim prepare to take her to God, she kisses each of the twins with "full, long kisses" (*Waters,* 297). The seraphim tell Sandy and

Dennys that their "love for Yalith, and hers for you, *is,* and therefore it always will be" (*Waters,* 300).

Sandy and Dennys return to the Murry house via unicorn and seraphim eager to resume their normal lives. They don't seem as profoundly changed by their otherworld experiences as Meg and Charles Wallace were by theirs. And yet though they are home, they can say that they will probably always be somewhat homesick for the world where they met a love that supplanted their pragmatism with faith.

Dance in the Desert

In *Dance in the Desert,* illustrated dramatically by Symeon Shimin, L'Engle uses the story of the holy family's trip to Egypt to explore the divinity and the humanity of the Christ child. In a narrative that in its sophistication may be more appropriate to young adults than to the typical readers of picture books, she presents a child who is simultaneously sovereign over the universe and vulnerable to the dangers of reality. The dance occurs in a moment out of time, or, to use L'Engle's distinctions, it occurs in *kairos*—eternal time— which in the narrative structure of this book is an interruption of *chronos*—chronometric time. In that moment, the parents and the other travelers in the caravan witness the natural authority that the child has over all created beings. The obeisance of each type of animal adds to the wonder of the scene, a mystery that culminates in the stately dance that is emblematic of L'Engle's view of reality, "a triumph of joy over fear."[5]

The story begins by noting the exceptional nature of the night of the dance, establishing a frame that highlights the mystery of the dance. The narrator does not say explicitly that it was a moment of eternal time, but merely implies that it was a time that was anything but ordinary:

> Once there was a night in the desert when nobody was afraid and everybody danced.
> This was an extraordinary night, because there is terror in the desert. (*Desert,* Spread One)[6]

This is an opening that mixes the comforting familiarity of a formulaic opening with the unsettling warning that the setting of the story is one that ought to inspire fear, a combination designed to intrigue readers to plunge into the story.

To emphasize the vulnerability of the holy family and to heighten the mysteriousness of the events that follow in the narrative, L'Engle uses the early pages of the book to develop the terror that is the normal reality of the desert. The narrator announces that the father does not "need to say aloud all that he knew there is to fear" (*Desert,* Spread One); the dangers are evident. What does not need saying are the dangers that lurk everywhere. L'Engle uses a series of vivid images built around active verbs to portray the dangers that the family is ever aware of. First there is the owl that "screams and rushes down" to grab its prey; then there is the eagle "that snatches the straying child"; and lurking everywhere, anywhere is the almost invisible lion that "stalks" and "leaps upon his unsuspecting prey" and the swift, malicious snake that "slithers," with its "jeweled eyes flashing," wondering "where shall the poison strike." There are scorpions, rats, spiders, and "wild asses with enormous, ludicrous, but frighteningly dangerous teeth" (*Desert,* Spread Two). But those, the next spread announces, are not the only dangers. Dragons—"some with wings like bats"—"lurk," waiting to attack the "unwary traveler." Even unicorns are rumored to be dangerous. And, as if animal dangers were not enough, there is the threat of bandits and of the desert itself. In short, the father knows that "A small family could never make it alone across the burning drifts, fiercely hot from the brazen sun by day, dunes cold as snow under the moon by night" (*Desert,* Spread Three).

But if the family is vulnerable to nature, it is also vulnerable to the whims of those who have the strength or the numbers to brave the terrors of the desert. In actions that can only be viewed ironically, given later history, caravan after caravan rejects the family. In the terms of the world in which they find themselves, the family is powerless and undesirable, inconsequential, perhaps even worthless. They are trapped between the desert and a king who is killing all the male children of the land in the hope of thereby destroying the Christ child. Even when one merchant does take pity on them because of the empathy he feels as a father, he is forced to address the complaints of his retinue who oppose being burdened with such problematic companions.

If the desert serves to demonstrate the vulnerability of the family, it also functions as a device to set them off from the rest of the world, thus setting the stage for the abnormal events at the center of the book. L'Engle emphasizes the way in which the desert separates the travelers from the rest of humanity, isolating them, but also consolidating them into a tighter community:

> The desert is like the ocean. It takes time to get out of the sight of land. And then suddenly there is nothing, nothing but waves of sand shifting and sliding in the wind, sand stretching out to eternity on every side. In the moonlight the fires and the tents and the camels make a small oasis for the travelers, and they draw in close, while the sands stir slowly around the caravan, spreading out into forever, and above them the stars break into distances beyond dreams. (*Desert,* Spread Six)

This lyrical presentation of the desert, linking the desert with the ocean and the stars, establishes a connection between the immediate situation of the caravan and the timeless context of the universe that surrounds it, setting the scene for the dance that occurs not in the *chronos* of the flight to Egypt but in *kairos*.

The metaphor of scene or stage is not inappropriate here, for in the events that follow, L'Engle crafts the narrative cinematically, often making the transition from the appearance of one animal to the appearance of the next on the basis of "sound cuts." In the first of these, we hear the roar of a lion from "outside the circle, from the edges of the dark" (*Desert,* Spread Seven). To the camel drivers, who throughout his section serve as foils to the Christ child and his family, the sound is a manifestation of the terror that stalks the desert in the night and they reach for their knives and reach to protect the child. Mary, however, prevents the driver from touching Jesus, and the lion and the child stand to face one another, each "holding out his arms in greeting" (*Desert,* Spread Eight). The amazed drivers discover not only that the lion brings no menace to the group, but that, in fact, it seems to ignore them completely, paying attention only to the child.

What follows is a dramatic progression of representative creatures great and small. Following the lion comes "a band of tiny desert mice" (*Desert,* Spread Ten). After the majestic and the tiny comes the grotesque, as L'Engle introduces "two enormous asses" with "a great idiotic bray" (*Desert,* Spread Eleven). In the silence after their ludicrous dance, the company hears the sound of great wings as three eagles descend to pay homage (*Desert,* Spread Twelve). And while all eyes are directed skyward to watch the dance of the birds, L'Engle sends a swift adder to curl "around the child's leg in sensuous swirls of affection" (*Desert,* Spread Fifteen). When the adder silently joins the circle of animals surrounding the camp, the scene changes again with the "irregular thudding" of ostriches that perform a cumbersome dance of their own.

The parade of homage points to the specialness and the authority of the child, but yet to this point in the narrative, L'Engle has not made any explicit revelation of his identity as the Christ child. That changes, however, with the entrances of the next creatures. L'Engle uses the typology of the unicorn and the pelican to reveal the identity of the recipient of all of this attention. The unicorn is the first creature to give notice to anyone beyond the child, and L'Engle has it lay its head in the mother's lap. L'Engle is evidently drawing on the medieval convention that unicorns are attracted to virgins, and she is clearly identifying the mother as the Virgin Mary (*Desert,* Spread Eighteen).[7] Immediately after the departure of the unicorn, a wounded pelican appears. The camel driver draws his knife to "put the bird out of its misery," but Mary stops him, recognizing, as does Jesus, that the pelican is a symbol of Christ and that the wound represents the mission of suffering that lies before the child. Mary cries without letting tears fall, and Jesus regards the pelican gravely. As if in mutual recognition of their similarities, "Bird and child looked at each other in silence (*Desert,* Spread Nineteen).[8] The identification of the child as Christ is complete when, upon the entrance of an owl and two dragons, Mary quotes the prophet Isaiah in a passage that anticipates the Messiah: "The dragons and the owls honor him . . . because he gives waters in the wilderness and rivers in the desert, and drink to his people (*Desert,* Spread Twenty).

The narrative culminates with a dance of all the creatures, a dance that, here as throughout L'Engle's work, reflects the orderliness of the universe. Like the dance of the universe in *Wind* and like the song of the stars in *Many Waters,* this dance is "stately" and "intricate." The dance expands, "the circle stretching, widening, until all the animals disappeared into the horizon, and the birds broke loose up into the sky" (*Desert,* Spread Twenty-two), rejoining the desert that L'Engle earlier had said was "stretching out to eternity on every side" (*Desert,* Spread Six).

As L'Engle shifts the narrative focus back to the desert, she shifts back to *chronos* as well. "No one had noticed," the narrator tells us, "when the child went back to his mother, but he was in her lap, sleeping, his arms flung out, his small hands open, fingers peacefully curled." The image is the traditional one of Madonna and child; "The mother's head was drooped over her child's; her arms lightly encircled him." The child is no longer independently and authoritatively at the center of activity as he was in the eternal moment. No longer functioning as the Christ, he is once again the child, and the family and caravan can only carry on in time, can only continue on to Egypt. The narrative concludes by stating simply, "The dance was over" (*Desert,* Spread Twenty-four), but for those who have witnessed the dance it will never really be over. Each witness has seen a bit of the mystery of the eternal, a moment of the *kairos* that exists beyond the *chronos.*

The Sphinx at Dawn

The two short stories in *The Sphinx at Dawn* pick up the life of the child and his parents in Egypt. In them, L'Engle develops familiar themes of the power of love and of the importance of responsible action as she explores the childhood of Yehoshuah. In both "Pakko's Camel" and "The Sphinx at Dawn," the young Christ is

essaying what it means to be the Messiah. As he discovers some of
the benefits and the costs of his station, he moves toward maturity.

In "Pakko's Camel," L'Engle uses the gift of the Magi as a symbol of the spiritual gifts that Yehoshuah possess. Given by the
wise men as their tribute to a future king, they are part of his des-
tiny. According to Yehoshuah's father the Magi told them that one
day the boy might have need of them. To conventional wisdom,
the gold, jewels, and precious oils represent great wealth, and
readers, like Yehoshuah's selfish friend Pakko, are likely to think
of the economic value of the gifts. But Yehoshuah isn't so certain
about the coffer that contains his legacy:

> When he was a little older he sometimes opened the door of the
> cupboard and looked questioningly at the coffer; but he did not
> open it, and he did not ask his mother or his father about it
> again. Something about the box disturbed him, and he felt in-
> stinctively that his parents would like it to be out of mind as
> well as out of sight. (*Sphinx,* 7)

What the parents no doubt find troubling about the box is its representation of that other part of their otherwise human son's nature. That box is a reminder of angels' visits, of dances in the
desert, of promises of the Messiah, promises that contained hints
of pain as well as assurances of salvation.

Yehoshuah finds his premonition partially justified when
Pakko, the only person to whom he has shown the treasure, steals
it. Yehoshuah then is faced with the difficult choice of what to do.
If he confronts Pakko directly, he realizes that Pakko will probably end up hating him and hating himself as well. Yet he cannot
ignore the other boy's action. As it is, through his visionary powers Yehoshuah can see that Pakko is angry at himself as well as at
the victim of his theft. Yehoshuah complains to the camel—which
L'Engle uses as a kind of medium for the spirit of God—"that it
seems . . . that there was death in that box" (*Sphinx,* 23).

L'Engle fashions Yehoshuah's dilemma so that he is forced to
realize the role of death in his gifts. Pakko's camel shows him a vision of two scenes that serve as prototypes of Yehoshuah's mis-

sion. In both, a prophet performs miracles that turn death into life. In one, Elisha revives the son of the Shunammite woman; in the other, Elijah breathes life into the son of the widow of Zarephath. Significantly, however, both of the sons in the vision appear to Yehoshuah as look-alikes of Pakko. When Yehoshuah returns to the village to discover that Pakko has suddenly died, the import of the vision is immediately evident.

Yehoshuah's lesson is to be obedient to his gifts. He had already discovered that he could "breathe life back into" small desert creatures (*Sphinx,* 27), and he imagines Pakko as one of those creatures. Such an act is not easy, however, and L'Engle crafts the passage to make it clear that the act was a somewhat painful exercise in obedience:

> Yos put his hand on Pakko's chest. It was motionless, silent. He held his hand over the heart. He whispered, "this is what I am asked to do isn't it?" He felt a pain in his own heart so intense that it crashed across his eyes. But he kept his hand on the cold, still chest. His lips moved: in the desert he often sang to himself the songs of David, and these words came to him now: "In the volume of the book it is written of me, that I would fulfill thy will, O my God: I am content to do it; yea, thy law is within my heart." (*Sphinx,* 28)

Yet hard as this act is, it is only part of the resuscitation of Pakko; it is only part of Yehoshuah's mission.

The larger task, according to the narrative, is to rescue Pakko from that death—that darkness—that he has brought upon himself by stealing Yehoshuah's treasure. That, as Yehoshuah muses after L'Engle has crafted events so that Pakko can return the treasure with impunity, is the more significant task of the Messiah:

> "A great miracle is easy to perform. To give life back to a body is no large thing. It is the other death, Pakko's camel, it is the other that is the darkness, and to put light in that darkness is...." He turned to the songs of David again, raising his face and his voice to the vast arc of sky: "For thou wilt light my candle: the Lord my God will enlighten my darkness. Unto thee, O Lord, will I lift up my soul. My God, I have put my trust in thee.

> I will always give thanks unto the Lord; his praise shall ever be
> in my mouth. O my God, my heart is ready, my heart is ready, I
> will sing and give praise." And as he sang, the heavy tiredness
> left him. (*Sphinx*, 30)

The mission of the Messiah is not physical but spiritual healing.
The gifts of the Magi, according to this story, were "useful" to
Yehoshuah, but in keeping with the paradoxical mission of the
Messiah, they were useful not as the world would expect them to
be useful, but they were useful in the occasion they provided for
Yehoshuah to exercise his real gifts.

L'Engle continues to explore the coming of age of the Messiah in
the title story of this volume. There she has Yehoshuah, accompanied again by another wise old camel, exchange riddles with the
sphinx. L'Engle combines the Greek tradition of the sphinx as
kingmaker with the Egyptian tradition of the sphinx as eternal
watcher of history. In his interactions with this symbol of human
time and kingdoms, Yehoshuah again demonstrates the strength
of his authority and the nonmaterial nature of his kingdom—the
kingdom of love.

Despite the apparent power and the manifest threat of the
sphinx, Yehoshuah faces him coolly, answering all the riddles accurately, revealing that he is not as other men. To demonstrate
that he is beyond the limitations of chronometric time, L'Engle
has him correctly answer a riddle that can only be answered with
lines from Shakespeare's *As You Like It* (*Sphinx*, 42). The only
riddle that somewhat troubles Yehoshuah is one that refers to his
own future. When the sphinx asks who was betrayed by a kiss,
Yehoshuah provides an answer out of Jewish history but experiences tremors of fear. Though he is divine, he is also human and
feels human emotions about the trials of his mission. But before
the boy leaves to, in the sphinx's words, "discover the kingdom of
which you are the prince" (*Sphinx*, 44), L'Engle has Yehoshuah
prove that he already possesses the essence of that kingdom.
When the sphinx queries what Yehoshuah has that the sphinx
will keep forever even after it has crumbled into sand, Yehoshuah
replies by kissing the sphinx and saying "You will keep my love"

(*Sphinx,* 46). L'Engle shows that even though he is limited by some of the normal human characteristics, Yehoshuah also contains the essence of divinity—unbounded love. "That is always your answer, isn't it?" says the sphinx, "The most difficult answer of all" (*Sphinx,* 46). These stories reveal that L'Engle's answer to that rhetorical question is "yes." For L'Engle, God is always love.

6. Coming of Age

The world of school was horrible. But then I would come home to
my room, where I would write and read and play the piano and
paint pictures. I lived in an interior world, and that was the real
world.

—"Unlikely Heroine"

Though they are not strictly autobiographical, three of L'Engle's early novels treat a matter that, as we have seen, was extremely significant in her own childhood—boarding school. After
L'Engle finished the third grade, her mother enrolled her in a private school for girls in New York despite the protests of her father.
The experience was to be a formative one; she was "miserably unhappy" in the new school and writes that she "learned nothing
more until [she] got to high school" ("Nourishment," 112). Her "de-
fense against the troubled, everyday world of [her] childhood" was
"to rely more and more on the private world that [she] discovered
in books" ("Nourishment," 112). If the experience lies behind her
early reading, it also lies behind her early writing. Boarding
school or the threat of it influences the plots of each of the novels
written in the 1940s and 1950s.

In each of these novels—*Camilla, And Both Were Young,* and
The Small Rain—a young woman is coming of age on her own.[1]

Each protagonist inhabits a world apart, a world set off from many normal social interactions, a world in which she is, for one reason or another, alienated from her parents. For Camilla Dickinson, Philippa Hunter, and Katherine Forrester, the world of adolescence is constrictive and repressive, yet at novel's end each has escaped that world in one way or another. For each, the narrative's conclusion represents a kind of beginning. Each stands on the verge of adulthood, cut off from her past with the world all before her.

Yet for all their similarities, the novels are not uniformly successful. While in *Camilla,* and in *And Both Were Young,* L'Engle creates plots that move the protagonists to maturity just as she does in *Rain,* she does so using conventional elements of romance fiction. As a result, those narratives are not as convincing as *Rain.* Just as romance fiction quite often "provides a fantasy solution to social conditions that are popularly accepted as insoluble," so the romance conventions of these plots provide fantasy fulfillment of the problems that the characters face (Cohn, 18).[2] L'Engle *does* use romantic relationships in the plot of *Rain,* but those relationships form only one part of the protagonist's coming of age. The result is characterization that is more realistic and a narrative that is more convincing.

Camilla

Camilla Dickinson's initiation into the world of adulthood comes as she confronts her parent's infidelity. Her awareness of their fallibility forces her to reflect on her own identity and values in relationship to theirs. In part, this reflection occurs through Camilla's expanding friendship with Luisa Rowan, a character that L'Engle uses as a worldly foil to the naïve Camilla. But in large part, Camilla's reflection and development occurs through her romantic relationship with Frank Rowan, Luisa's brother. Frank stands as the typical hero of the romance novel, and his developing relationship with Camilla forms the essence of the plot which, per the conventions of the period, builds around the question of whether the two lovers will kiss.

At the beginning of the novel, Camilla's father discovers her mother in an afternoon tryst with her lover, Jacques Nissen. That affair and Rafferty Dickinson's discovery of it makes Camilla a pawn in the battle between her parents. Caught in the middle of this complex emotional game, Camilla becomes more and more isolated, increasingly forced to discover her own emotional support. With similarly disastrous results, each of the adults in the triangle separately interrogates her and tries to win her allegiance. Her father, whom she apparently rarely sees, takes her to dinner to question her and to try to influence her, but what he communicates is his miscomprehension of Camilla. He is uncertain of her age, he unsettles her by joking suggestively about their relationship, and he encourages her to have a drink that makes her ill. Camilla's mother, in turn, probes Camilla about her conversation with her father, obviously essaying her allegiance and warning her that love can be killed in the same breath with which she tells the girl that she loves her. Camilla's alienation and confusion is compounded the following day when her mother attempts suicide. But perhaps the final straw breaks when Jacques asks her to understand her mother's need for attention and affection from him. Camilla's response is one that she says she utters because she wants to believe in it, not because she knows it to be true. She retorts to Jacques that it is not a child's responsibility to nurture her mother but a mother's reponsibility to nurture a daughter.

Camilla moves from hating her mother for her continued interest in Jacques to hating the situation. She wanders the streets of New York thinking about her problem and yearning for the simplicity of childhood:

> ... suddenly I was so tired that my legs were ready to collapse under me, and I wanted my mother. I did not want Rose Dickinson who had been talking on the telephone to Jacques Nissen. I want my mother. I want my mother to come and take me by the hand and lead me home and undress me and put me to bed and rub my head and bring me milk toast and then turn out my light but leave the door open with the light from the hall shining in and sit by my bed and hold my hand until I fell asleep. . . .
> But Mother was still in bed with her wrists bound in white ban-

dages and the telephone beside her so that in the end she could
not help talking to Jacques. (*Camilla,* 93)

The cadence of the prose with its short statements of want linked
by the conjunction "and" emphasizes Camilla's need to be loved.
Unfairly pulled out of the only relationship that has provided
emotional nurture, she is alone and vulnerable.

But just when Camilla is at this emotional nadir, L'Engle
brings in Frank, who functions as a conventional romantic hero.
Mentally calling upon her Mother, Camilla wonders where she
can go and continues to wander the streets again. Though she
says that she does not pay attention to where she is wandering,
she is not shocked that she ends up in front of Frank's house. Neither, of course, is the reader, who recognizes the romance plot
that begins with Camilla's introduction to Frank the day before.
After that meeting, Camilla's mind was consumed with thoughts
of Frank as only the mind of a romantic heroine could be. "All the
way home," she recalls, "I thought about the way he had told me I
was beautiful, and the way he had put his hands on my shoulders
and told me we were having a date, and the way he had held my
hand when we said good-bye" (*Camilla,* 66). If on that first occasion Frank demonstrates the sensitivity of the romantic hero by
understanding Camilla just as she needed to be understood, he
now demonstrates his heroic manliness and strength by taking
complete charge of her. Without telling her where he is taking
her, he grasps her arm and walks her so rapidly that she almost
has to run to keep up, but Camilla does not care. "All that mattered," she tells us, "was that Frank had my arm and that he was
taking care of me" (*Camilla,* 95). He takes her to an old movie theater where they can talk, stopping only momentarily in the lobby
so that he can be a knight-in-shining-armor to an immigrant
woman who cannot get the candy machine to work. But finally
they do talk and Frank does help her. In their conversation,
Camilla expresses what for her is an emotional truth, if not an
empirical fact—her mother is dead. Replacing her is Frank.

And in some ways a young woman could not have a better replacement than Frank, or at least so Camilla thinks. In her eyes,
he is different from the other young men. As she thinks about the

way her peers talk with their dates, she is certain that their con-
versations could not possibly be as stimulating or as thrilling as
hers with Frank because none of the young men she had ever met
talked at all the way he did. L'Engle shows them laughing and
talking a lot, but not just conversing about superficial things.
They quickly move to a significant level of conversation, a development that is another important ingredient in the romance formula. But Camilla and Frank do not merely talk about God,
truth, and life—they *agree* on these topics. When Frank confesses
his belief that God had nothing to do with a close friend's suicide,
Camilla fairly explodes in her recognition of their affinity. "I
wanted to cry out for joy," she exclaims. "Oh, yes! We believe in
the same God!" (*Camilla,* 165). That fact removes all of the previous confusion from Camilla's mind. Frank seems to embody the
most vital attribute of the romantic hero; he is special, different
from other men.

But the danger in the romance is that the hero's apparent specialness is really a mask that covers his philandering. "The romance hero," notes one critic, "is very often a man with a past, a
dark history of involvement" with other women (Cohn, 48). L'Engle introduces that tension into the plot by her mention of Frank's
other women, particulary Pompilia Riccioli, who haunts the narrative, raising questions in the reader's mind about Frank's sincerity. Pompilia appears in the theater lobby during that all-
important moment when Frank is consoling Camilla, and though
she is with a date of her own, she calls Frank "honey" (*Camilla,*
99). And then Luisa, Frank's sister and Camilla's friend, warns
Camilla about Frank's somewhat fickle attitude toward relationships. Luisa claims that Frank never lets a relationship last more
than a couple of months and notes that his fling with Pompilia
Riccioli—which lasted three months—was unusually long in its
duration. Camilla knows that Luisa may have been trying to hurt
her by telling her this, yet enough people mention Pompilia to
make Camilla "hate the name of Pompilia Riccioli" and to wonder
about her own status with Frank (*Camilla,* 196). Even Frank,
when confronted by Pompilia's father in front of Camilla has the
bravado to avow that he procures a new girl "every week," but he

asserts, with a kind of macho wink, that Riccioli's daughter is still the "queen" (*Camilla*, 218). This tension adds to that of the building romance, making Camilla play close attention to the nuances of Frank's behavior.

Despite Camilla's obvious concern about her relationship with Frank, L'Engle limits her to the passive behavior of the romantic heroine. Her only option *is* to carefully watch Frank, to listen for significant cues. When, for example, Frank mentions doing something with her during the coming summer, Camilla breathes a sigh of relief, thinking to herself that if Frank thinks of her in this fairly long-term fashion she must be more to him than "just another Pompilia Riccioli" (*Camilla*, 220). But Camilla's problem is compounded by Frank's behavior. Like the typical romantic hero, he is moody, unpredictable, violent (Cohn, 42). When in that moment in the theater Camilla says that she lacks the will to live, Frank shakes her until her teeth chatter in her head and she starts to cry. He apologizes, but even then his voice is "shaky with rage" and he blames Camilla for his violence: "you made me do it. You made me" (*Camilla*, 98). Camilla's response to his violence is to accept it, to wait for Frank to hold her hand again so that she can know that "it was all right between us again" (*Camilla*, 99).

The psychologically perceptive reader has to recognize unresolved issues and misdirected anger in Frank's violent outbursts, but Camilla lacks the sophistication to perceive such causes. Her passivity is not surprising then, if her suggestion that Frank get something to eat can elicit the following kind of response:

> "Me, you think I could eat?" Frank turned on me and his voice was suddenly savage. "You think I could eat when the minute you're born you're condemned to die? When thousands of people are dying every minute before they've even had a chance to begin? Death isn't fair. It's—it's denial of life. How can we be given life when we're given death at the same time? Death isn't fair, . . . I resent death! I resent it with every bone in my body! And you think—you think I could eat!" (*Camilla*, 253)

The mood passes, but Frank never apologizes for this verbal abuse; instead, Camilla feels as though he looks at her as though he hates her, as though she repels him. She is predictably passive in the remainder of her dealings with him. If L'Engle makes him the stereotypical male character in his inability to communicate, she makes Camilla a stereotypical female.

Behind Frank's anger is his experience with the brokenness of the world, particularly through his relationships with two male friends—one who committed suicide and another, David, who lost his legs in World War II. L'Engle explains that Frank's "passion for peace" was her response to the Red scares of the fifties (*Two-Part*, 135). Such events, however, didn't exist in Camilla's childhood world, and L'Engle uses Frank to expand her horizons. Though what she discovers is far from pretty, Camilla is grateful for Frank's influence. Her friendship with Luisa had given her a kind of telescope with which to see new worlds, but that friendship did not offer nearly as much as hers with Frank: "Frank's telescope," she declares, "was much stronger than Luisa's" (*Camilla*, 202). Part of the attraction of Frank for Camilla is the allure of the new world of experience that he can introduce her to. Because it belongs to the hero and because he typically offers, after some initial reluctance, to share it with the heroine, that new world—however harsh or ugly—makes her old world unappealing.

As Camilla turns more and more toward Frank for comfort and guidance, she looks more and more for the sign that will signal his love and his sincerity—the kiss. The plot develops expectantly toward that moment with episodes in which Frank *almost* kisses her. In the most memorable one, the two lovers are walking home in the snow when suddenly Frank stops and says her name. There is a moment as they stand there that Camilla comes to recall as a timeless moment, a moment when they stand cheek to cheek and in which Camilla could feel Frank's heart making a "strong swift thumping" against her chest (a phenomenon that given their winter attire seems rather remarkable). But since Frank does not actually kiss her here, Camilla has to decide what to make of this episode. She still wonders if she was merely one of Frank's girls, but yet she feels too happy to believe that. When she resolves that tension in a dream in which Frank actually does kiss her, she is convinced that she wants him to kiss her "more than anything in the world" (*Camilla,* 208).

From that moment on the reader is waiting for the culmination of their love. The expectation of the kiss is present whenever the two are together. Camilla is tested when Frank's friend David kisses her and passionately terms her his "untarnished, unawakened little Camilla" (*Camilla,* 229). He is hardly the "dastardly villain" that critics have identified as a regular character of the conventional romance (Cawelti, 270), yet his function in the narrative is similar, providing at least some slight competition for the hero.[3] After his kiss, Camilla noticeably broods until she suddenly knows that the moment in the snow with Frank "had been much more important than David's kiss" (*Camilla,* 231). That decision again heightens the anticipation of the kiss, but since Camilla is stuck in a passive role, she cannot utter what she feels, and the anticipation becomes great when in another moment alone with Frank she confesses to the reader that suddenly with Frank she "felt the same warm glow" that she had felt when David touched her, and she desperately wants to cry, "Oh, Frank, kiss me, kiss me" (257) Such expressive passion, however, lies outside the realm of appropriate feminine behavior.

Instead she must be content with Frank's embrace and his declarations of fidelity. When the two discover that circumstances are going to separate them—Camilla to boarding school and Frank to a different city—Frank makes his strongest statement of commitment. He tells her that she *is* special, that he feels differently about her than other women, that he talks differently to her than to other women. Such a declaration, of course, is the fulfillment of Camilla's dreams. As she muses on it afterwards she grows weak in the knees just thinking of the way Frank held her, and it is not until she goes to bed that night that she recalls that Frank had not kissed her. She remembers that, however, without regret, as though the embrace and the declaration were sign enough.

In the climactic chapter of the novel, however, her dream is shattered when, despite his declaration of love and, indeed, despite specific plans for the next day, Frank leaves town, apparently jilting Camilla. When Frank is gone without saying goodbye, what has happened seems evident. All Frank's heroic sensitivity was a hoax. His declaration of fidelity was merely manipulation. To Frank Rowan, Camilla Dickinson was merely another Pompilia Riccioli. All the romantic conventions seem to have been shattered with Camilla's dreams. Yet at the very end of the narrative, L'Engle salvages the romance with a note. Out of jealousy, Luisa initially had not delivered a brief missive from Frank explaining his actions. In it he explains that he cannot say good-bye and cannot explain why. Camilla will "just have to know" (*Camilla,* 277), just as she earlier just had to accept his violence. To the very end he is the moody romantic hero who cannot honestly articulate his feelings or easily make an emotional commitment. He signs the note "Love, Frank," but the word *love* is scribbled "in a hurried, shaky way, as though it was a difficult word for him to write" (*Camilla,* 277).

It is not unusual for a romance plot to end with the separation of the lovers, particularly if it is done as L'Engle does it here, "in such a way as to suggest that the love relation has been of lasting and permanent impact" (Cawelti, 42). Frank's letter makes all the difference for Camilla, for with it she can sustain the memory of their love. Though she is still deeply hurt by the separation, she keeps the letter as a talisman of Frank. She does not have him, but she has this missive to look at, to hold to. The letter helps her to go on with life; she is sadder, but stronger. In one sense, Camilla has matured beyond the world of her parents, but in another sense, because her experience has been only the passive experience of the conventional romantic heroine, she has not matured at all. Her identity and her sense of self-worth are dependent on her memory of her relationship with the more powerful male hero.

And Both Were Young

Camilla Dickinson does not become Philippa Hunter, the protagonist of *And Both Were Young,* yet there is a sense in which this

novel picks up where *Camilla* leaves off, for its plot arises out of
the unhappy boarding school experience of its protagonist, an experience that in the foreword to the novel, L'Engle identifies as
similar to her own. But again, if, as in *Camilla,* L'Engle draws on
autobiographical material, she was not writing an autobiographical novel. Her experience may have led to the inclusion of certain
incidents and contributed to certain aspects of setting or character. However, by and large, as in *Camilla,* the plot is the plot
of the popular romance, a fact that has caused one reviewer of
the revised edition (in which L'Engle claims to restore some of the
frankness about sex and death that had been edited out of
the 1949 edition) to term this an "old-fashioned" novel.[4] Like
Camilla, Philippa begins the novel alienated from her parents
and isolated from the rest of the world, and like Camilla, Philippa
is transported from her world of trouble by a romantic relationship that some see as "brisk and lively"; still—because of its formulaic nature—it offers only a fantasy solution to her problems.[5]

Philippa's problems are immediately evident. Her mother was
killed in an automobile accident the year before and her father, an
artist, is seeing a woman of whom Philippa does not approve. In
part, her disapproval is connected to her love for her mother.
Philippa sees this Eunice Jackman as opportunistic. "You'd have
thought she was just waiting for mother to die," Philippa complains, "the way she moved in" (*And Both,* 4). Philippa admits
that Jackman is superficially nice, but from her perspective, the
older woman behaves so just to get to Philippa's father. The worst
part of the situation for Philippa is that she is being separated
from her father, a problem she blames on Jackman:

> I'm being sent to boarding school, and it's all because of Eunice
> Jackman wanting me out of the way so she can get her claws
> into Father. He'd never have thought of making me go away to
> school if Eunice hadn't persuaded him it was—what did she
> say?—inappropriate—for me to travel around with him while
> he makes sketches for a book. (*And Both,* 5)

Philippa feels misunderstood and trapped by her circumstances.
When she sees a steamer crossing the Swiss lake where she is

staying just prior to boarding school, she wishes that she could get on the boat "and just ride and ride forever and ever" (*And Both,* 5).

Since she cannot escape, she romantically imagines that, like the hero of Lord Byron's "The Prisoner of Chillon," she will be a prisoner at the boarding school. She begins the narrative as a child and so when she thinks of rescue, she imagines that it is her father who will at the Christmas holidays rescue her from her imprisonment. And while initially her father promises to do so, L'Engle substitutes someone else for her father. Philippa ultimately is rescued from her prison, as she defines it, but she is rescued by her romantic relationship with a handsome young man living at a chateau next to the boarding school. Over the course of the novel, Philippa transfers her dependence from her father to her lover.

The boarding school is not quite a prison, but to a young person used to privacy and freedom, it understandably seems confining. But L'Engle makes it clear that while some aspects of Philippa's situation are objectively repressive, others are subjective—a kind of imprisonment that Philippa makes for herself.

The objective elements of repression are obvious. The school identifies students by number, not by name. Philippa and the other students are not permitted to answer the matron's questions casually. Each response must be submissively polite and include the matron's name: "Yes, Miss Tulip" instead of a simple "yes" (*And Both,* 26). The school affords the girls no privacy; even bathing is timed and subject to inspection. But worst of all, from Philippa's perspective, are the ways in which both the teachers and the girls misunderstand and humiliate her. Teachers publicly chide her for her clumsiness, and her peers pick her last when choosing teams for sports or other activities. She is so oppressed by the lack of privacy that she can say that she knows "ultimately and forever how the caged animals constantly stared at in the zoo must feel" (*And Both,* 34).

Though she portrays the repressiveness of the institution, L'Engle also identifies a portion of Philippa's problem in the young girl's penchant to feel sorry for herself. Philippa is forced to acknowledge that some of the walls of her prison are psychological when the one teacher she respects confronts her about her attitude. "I know you're not happy here, Philippa," chides Madame Perceval, "but when you make it so easy for the girls to tease you, you can't blame them for taking advantage of it. Girls can be very cruel, especially when they get the idea that someone is different" (*And Both,* 95). When Philippa protests that she *is* different, that she is tall and clumsy, Perceval becomes "really severe": "I didn't expect to hear you talk quite so foolishly, Philippa. You are tall, yes, but you can turn that into an advantage later on. And perhaps right now you're a little awkward, but you'll outgrow that" (*And Both,* 95). Confronted by the fact that the most popular girl in one of the classes wears a leg brace, Philippa is forced to acknowledge her own self-pity. She realizes what Paul's father would later observe, that she wants "to be exactly like everybody else and yet be different at the same time" (*And Both,* 123).

But whether the walls of her prison are objectively or subjectively real, Philippa is a heroine ripe for rescue by the right kind of hero. And from the first page of the novel when Philippa literally bumps into the handsome French youth, it is obvious to the reader, if not to the heroine, who that rescuer will be. Paul has all the qualifications for the job. He is handsome and noble-looking, reminding Philippa of a page that she had seen in a tapestry. Both have "the same unselfconscious grace" and "the same self-assured nobility," and like Paul, "the page was tall and slender with huge dark eyes and thick hair" (*And Both,* 87). If Paul has an air of nobility, he also has the mysterious origins of the romantic hero. Paul cannot remember his true name or his biological parents, a fact that dovetails nicely with the romantic convention of the hidden prince. But most importantly, Paul is sensitive and supportive. From that first chance meeting, he proves that he has a knack for understanding Philippa. When Philippa is with him she senses "that he would prefer someone whose words were clumsy and inadequate, but honest, to someone whose words were glib and superficial" (*And Both,* 82).

The plot, then, develops the story of her rescue by Paul from her psychological prison. In part, just knowing him and being able to get away from the school on occasion to see him constitutes a release for Philippa. She is sustained by "the glorious secret knowledge of Paul" (*And Both,* 144). But since some of her psychological imprisonment was caused by public humiliation, her release needs to be public as well. The incident that causes Phillippa the greatest public pain is her banishment from the school's ski races because the ski teacher finds her clumsy and difficult to teach. Paul rescues her by secretly teaching her until she is good enough to surprise her peers and win the race. Though Philippa does not actually win the event (because she stops to aid an injured comrade), she does win the cup given to the most improved skier and is vindicated in the eyes of her world.

As the plot moves toward this affirmation of Philippa, the only real tension comes from the threat of Paul's removal from the scene. In a modern variation on the convention of the hidden prince, L'Engle shapes Paul as a hero who has forgotten his name and his past because of the war. It is a plausible menace, then, when after their love has been sealed by their first kiss, a mysterious stranger arrives claiming to be Paul's father and threatening to take him away. This character, a stereotypical villain—"a dark man with the too-brilliant black eyes" (*And Both,* 174)—imperils their relationship not only by raising the possibility of Paul's elimination from Philippa's life, but also by sullying the apparent nobility of Paul's character. What if Paul's background were as shabby and ignoble as this man who makes Philippa "sick from distaste and loathing" (*And Both,* 175)?

The romance formula wouldn't, of course, permit a hero with such a background. And, indeed, Paul turns out to be a hero with the best of postwar pedigrees—his parents were in the Resistance and were killed in a concentration camp. But L'Engle does not reveal that until after a bit of melodrama in which Philippa masquerades as Paul and meets with the villain in an effort to protect Paul. When, in that rendezvous, Philippa is injured, Paul regains his memory. The image of Philippa lying hurt on the chateau floor triggers the memory of his sister who had been shot by the Nazis. But the entire episode is so tidily packaged that it seems contrived just to move the plot along and to introduce a degree of tension in the narrative.

Philippa's victory brings the narrative to conclusion; she has been redeemed in the eyes of the world and released from her prison. The ostensible moral of the narrative is "that the freedom was in herself, just as the prison had been" (*And Both,* 240), but to say that is to say something a bit different from what the narrative itself says. The structure of the narrative suggests that Philippa's freedom has come from her relationship with Paul. She does learn something about denying self-pity through the events of the story, but even that lesson is dependent on the self-confidence she draws from her relationship with Paul. From the moment that they bump into each other at the start of the narrative to the moment that they walk offstage hand in hand at the conclusion, it is clear that the primary way that Philippa grows is through her dependence on the male hero.

The Small Rain

At first glance, *The Small Rain* seems to employ many of the same strategies of plot and characterization as these other two novels. A youthful protagonist isolated from parents and friends begins the narrative. She survives the repressive life of a Swiss boarding school, and finishes the story in a conclusion that is as much a beginning as it is an ending. Yet *Rain,* which L'Engle wrote earlier than either *Camilla* or *And Both,* is more successful than either of the other two novels because of the complexity of its plot and characterization. While romantic love certainly enters the plot of *Rain,* it does not drive the plot as it does in the other novels. As a result, *Rain* is a less formulaic, more honest and complex novel than either *Camilla* or *And Both,* a novel that was enthusiastically received when it appeared in 1945 and which was also well received in 1984 when it was reissued.[6] The romance that we see at the end of *Rain,* is that of a young woman looking ahead to the decade of her twenties, confronted with a significant choice: "to stay the course as a serious artist or to compromise her work for love."[7]

At the start of *Rain,* Katherine Forrester, the protagonist, is a 10-year-old girl wandering through the world of adults. Her mother, Julie, a concert pianist, has been injured in an automobile accident three years before, leaving Katherine to live with an aunt, Manya Sergeievna, a famous actress. Theater life is exciting but lonely for Katherine. We see her confiding to one of the actors something that she never has confided to her aunt—that she finds it difficult to have a mother but yet to be prevented from seeing her. As loved as she is in her situation with her aunt, she desperately craves the affection of a parent.

L'Engle grants Katherine's desire; she is reunited with her mother, but the familial world that she finds herself in is hardly the secure world of the Austins or the Murrys. As she experiences the joy of reunion with her mother, she also has to come to terms with the brokenness that is a reality of her world. She has to face the reality of her father's affair with her Aunt Manya and all that that entails. She has to face the fallibility and complexity of the adults in her life. She has to face her mother's bitterness about the loss of her performance career and her resultant alcoholism. Her life is still a life of theaters and bars; she regains her mother, but not her childhood.

As much as she might yearn for security, the events of Katherine's life provide just the opposite. At 14, after four happy, if not always easy, years with her mother, Katherine is forced once more into a role beyond her years when her mother dies. On the surface, Katherine deals with the death matter-of-factly, but beneath the surface, her wounds are evident. As her mother lies dying, she makes a prayer that reveals her need for security and love:

> She said over and over again in her mind—God, please make mother be all right, dear God, please make my mother be all right—until the words stopped making sense and got all jumbled, and she found herself saying—Mother, please make my God be all right. (*Rain*, 56)

In those jumbled words, L'Engle captures the essence of a child's need, for if her mother should die, could she truly say that God is all right? When her mother does die, Katherine's hurt is evident in the way she isolates herself from all human contact. She lies to elude helpful friends and avoids any physical contact because "she didn't want to be held by anyone, to feel anyone's body against hers, to get comfort from any human being" (*Rain*, 58). The threat of death becomes part of Katherine's reality, so much so that later when she sees a lake and mountains hidden by fog, she wonders if they still exist. After all, she muses, "people died and were never seen again" (*Rain*, 97).

As she deals with her loss, her mother becomes an ideal figure for her. She forgets the difficulties of their relationship so that even the images of her mother's depression and her alcoholism dim in her memory. Though she recognizes the danger of playing the piano merely for her mother's sake, she nonetheless attacks the instrument with rigorous discipline as though to do justice to the memory of her mother, and she asserts that she is going to be a pianist like her mother. As she thinks of herself, she doubts that she "can ever be strong and wonderful" like her Mother (*Rain*, 62), but what is significant is that she is trying. When she wants to succumb to her pain and cry, she does not because, as she tells a friend, "Mother said I musn't give in to things" (*Rain*, 66).

Part of the power of this novel is the psychological complexity with which L'Engle imbues the characters. The question of pain and the problem of death will hover over Katherine for the entire novel, but L'Engle does show moments of respite, moments that realistically show Katherine's gradual healing. In one such moment, Katherine experiences the balm of natural beauty that gives her a peace that she has not felt since her mother's death. On this particular evening she has taken a walk to see the sunset, but has come too late and is filled with an irrational anger. She finds that she wants to wail "Why couldn't you wait! Why couldn't you wait!" at the sun, though no doubt the cry would be as much directed at her mother as at the sun (*Rain*, 69). In her anger she runs blindly into the woods until she comes to a spot that is almost magical in its beauty. She falls onto a bed of moss in a circle of toadstools next to a pool. As she lies in this fairy ring, Katherine experiences her first healing:

> For the first time since Julie's death she felt a kind of peace that was not the nervous hypnotism of her work at the piano, but that seemed to reach all the way inside her and suddenly

made her exhaustion a simple thing, almost beautiful, because now she could close her eyes and sleep. (*Rain,* 70)

For her as for Vicki Austin, beauty brings an answer to the problem of pain.

Julie's death, however, has forced Katherine into a kind of false adulthood in which she denies her real emotions, denies her real age. Her father and her aunt, now married, take her in but she resists their affection. Though it was not easy, she fought "against the warm blanket of love and tenderness and pity they were constantly throwing over her . . . when all she wanted was coldness" (*Rain,* 68). But she is not able to resist the warmth or hang on to this false maturity for long. Again, L'Engle uses beauty to bring healing, this time through art—through a song sung by Katherine's Aunt Manya. As her aunt sings, Katherine experiences an emotional change that is accompanied by a physical sensation of warmth. After listening to several songs, Katherine is able to identify the emotion that she has denied herself. She realizes that this warm feeling is love, and she permits herself to reenter a youthful world of protection and happiness.

The suspension of her emotional independence also marks a return to vulnerability. L'Engle concludes one chapter with this happy scene, but begins the very next in a narrative voice that conveys Katherine's sense of betrayal: "But they sent her to boarding school, her father and Aunt Manya, to an English boarding school in Switzerland" (*Rain,* 92). Her use of the appositive phrase to identify this *they* that was sending her off emphasizes her hurt; it as much as asks how these can be the same people by whom she felt so loved. Being a teenager as opposed to being an adult means being subject to the wishes of adults. She had let go of her pain, let go of her attempt to achieve adulthood to no avail. She complains that "the years had rolled off her" but that it is "no help" (*Rain,* 92). Instead of feeling surrounded by the "warm blanket" of love, she finds herself surrounded by the cold fog that envelops the school.

When Katherine discovers life in the school to be as suffocating as that fog, she again draws strength from the romantic ideal of her mother. The other girls shun her, and the rules oppress her. She loses the one friend she has when the school staff accuse them of developing a lesbian relationship. However, when she discovers a piano teacher—Justin Vigneras—who understands her, her perception of the world changes. Music and the music studio represent a romantic escape for her. She is free to use his studio in her spare time and the place becomes a symbolic world for her. It is a place apart, a place of romance and art, a place that reminds her of her mother's world. From this point on, reality is divided for Katherine into the artistic world—Julie's world or Justin's world, as she often terms it—and the other, more mundane world.

Her attitude toward Justin and his world seems ripe for development in terms of the conventional romance. But L'Engle does not succumb to that temptation. She toys with conventions. They are there in Katherine's breathless attention to Justin's every movement. They are there when on a covert trip to Paris, the two of them drink too much wine and then kiss. But they disappear when Katherine realizes that it was not she "that he kissed," that "she was just the person who was there," that "it would have been whoever was there" (*Rain*, 21). They disappear when Justin leaves the school. L'Engle keeps Justin on Katherine's mind, but she does so realistically, not formulaically. Justin has captured the romantic part of Katherine's imagination, but as L'Engle develops her character, there are other significant aspects to her imagination and her life, just as there is much more to the plot than their relationship.

L'Engle brings Katherine to maturity by putting her through real life—through situations that are not always easy, and which do not, perhaps, have an obvious moral, situations that are somehow typical of adult life. Katherine's first is a sexual affair with Charlot, a kind of foster son of her aunt's. As Katherine analyzes the sexual liaison the morning after, L'Engle's intent to break from stereotypical patterns of feminine behavior is clear. Katherine muses that sex is not very important unless you make it a soulful gift or unless you let it cheapen you, neither of which she has done in this instance, she believes. In her analytical distance and careful control, her response is that of the modern feminist,

not of the conventional heroine. In fact, when Charlot makes traditional noises about love, she tells him that he does not need to
say anything, and that he is just making his declarations of love
"because of what happened last night" (*Rain,* 199). She is even
willing to face being a single mother, though she acknowledges it
would be difficult. Her lesson, if there is one beyond what she already has discerned, is biblical, though not a message of sin or ret-
ribution. Manya reads her this passage from the Book of Acts:
"We glory in tribulations also: know that tribulation worketh patience; and patience, experience; and experience, hope."

An incident that is hard to understand, except in terms of what it
offers Katherine in experience, is the death of a schoolmate—Pene-
lope Deerenforth. Though she does not know her well, Katherine
accompanies Pen to Paris where she is to meet her fiancé and his
family. While there, Katherine learns that Charlot, too, is engaged,
and her hurt over his not informing her suggests that their sexual
intimacy carried more of a legacy than she was willing initially to
admit. But the hardest lesson for Katherine appears when Pen,
walking in her sleep, steps through a third-story window to her
death. "Nobody's safe!" Katherine cries out. "It's all around, reaching out for you, catching you unawares" (*Rain,* 241). She believes
that she is supposed to use such experience, but it is hard for her to
believe that she is going to "live long enough to be able to make use
of the things that have happened" to her (*Rain,* 249).

But perhaps the most significant step in Katherine's process of
maturity occurs upon her return to the States to study with her
mother's old piano teacher. There she falls into a bohemian life-
style with a group of friends and becomes engaged to the man who
was her stage friend back when she was 10. The relationship
brings Katherine a joy that she has not had for much of her life.
She stands before the mirror and says "Look, Katherine. This is
happiness. This is what being happy is really like. Do not be un-
conscious of it for a single minute" (*Rain,* 293). Thus her pain is
the more intense when her fiancé leaves her for Sarah, her friend
and roommate. In her despair she even fantasizes about suicide,
imagining how her body would hit the cement walk below her
apartment.

What she does with this pain depends very much on her maturity. And what she *does* do with it proves her maturity. She cries and lets go of it:

> She felt as though she had been in great pain, as though she had been lost in it, had ceased to be Katherine Forrester and become part of the pain. But now she was herself again. She was Katherine. And although the pain was still there, it no longer possessed her. No, she possessed it; it was part of her; she could enclose everything in the span of her mind and heart. (*Rain,* 369)

Her deliverance, her maturity, is different from Camilla Dickinson's or Philippa Hunter's. Hers is not dependent on a man. She looks forward to seeing Justin again, but she does so as a result of her maturity and not because he has been her guide toward that end. Because we have seen her move from tribulation to experience we can accept her hope in L'Engle's lyrical conclusion. As she travels aboard a ship bound for Europe, Katherine lies there, "under the stars, under the wind, under the vastness of the universe, while land became lost in the September night, and water reached out, illimitable, mysterious, on all sides" (*Rain,* 371). Whereas in *And Both,* L'Engle needs to tell us that this is not an ending but a beginning, here we do not need to be told. Because of the realistic development of plot and character, we can feel the authenticity of Katherine's emotions.

Afterword

> God created, and it was joy: time, space, matter. There *is*, and
> we are part of that is-ness, part of that becoming. That is our
> calling: co-creation. Every single one of us, without exception, is
> called to co-create with God. No one is too unimportant to have a
> share in the making or unmaking of the final showing forth.
> Everything that we do either draws the Kingdom of love closer,
> or pushes it further off. That is a fearful responsibility, but when
> God made 'man in our image, male and female,' responsibility
> went with it. Too often we want to let somebody else do it, the
> preacher, or the teacher, or the government agency. But if we
> are to continue to grow in God's image, then we have to accept
> the responsibility.
>
> —*And It Was Good*

After reviewing L'Engle's work as we have done, what finally
can be said? Critics often desire to place authors in niches, to offer
definitive statements of their lasting merit. If awards could serve
as a means of evaluation, L'Engle would score highly. She has received many: the Newbery Medal and the Newbery Honor Award;
the American Book Award and the Austrian State Prize; the
Regina Medal and the University of Southern Mississippi Medal-
lion; and the list could go on. Yet a number of critics have termed
her writing pedantic or uneven, several referring to an assess-

ment made by John Rowe Townsend in which he has asserted that L'Engle is "a curiously-gifted, curiously learned, curiously-imperfect writer."[1] Surprisingly, L'Engle might not quibble with the spirit of that assessment, especially if she would be permitted to define what *perfect* means and to substitute that word for Townsend's *imperfect*. *Perfect*, according to L'Engle, is a Latin term that means "to do thoroughly," an action that she equates with being human: "not infallible or impeccable or faultless, but human" ("Heroic," 124). Her notion of what it means to be perfect, then, meshes with what Townsend has intended by his term *imperfect*. It is in this sense that L'Engle desires perfection for herself and her fictional characters; she wants her protagonists to be perfect, "defining perfect as thorough, thoroughly human, making mistakes, sometimes doing terrible things through wrong choices, but ultimately stretching themselves beyond their limitations" ("Heroic," 124).

The importance of L'Engle's fiction for young adults rests in exactly this—in her willingness to address the whole range of human experience in her fiction, to write about pain as well as joy, to essay despair as well as hope. But the real power of her fiction is that in addressing the difficult issues that young adults—that all of us, really—face; she does not, as many contemporary writers do, neglect the spiritual dimension of human experience. The result is a corpus of fiction that ultimately demonstrates what M. Sarah Smedman has called the "triumph of the spirit," a collection of books "which courageously embrace an unwashed world and incarnate its dirtiness, ugliness, and festering sores, yet transmit the conviction that there is some meaning, some justice, some goodness in the face of so much contrary evidence."[2] But justice and goodness do not occur by themselves in a broken world. The novels point to the importance of choosing good over evil, of exercising moral responsibility, of working on the side of love.

Notes

Preface

1. Frederick Buechner, *The Clown in the Belfry: Writings on Faith and Fiction* (San Francisco: HarperCollins, 1992) 86–87.

Chapter One

1. *Walking on Water: Reflections on Faith and Art* (Wheaton, Ill.: Shaw, 1980), 53; hereafter cited in text as *Walking*.
2. *Two-Part Invention: The Story of a Marriage* (New York: Farrar, Straus and Giroux, 1988), 5; hereafter cited in text as *Two-Part*.
3. *Camilla* (1951; reprint, New York: Delacorte, 1965); hereafter cited in text as *Camilla*.
4. "The Heroic in Literature and in Living," *The Lion and the Unicorn* 13:1 (1989), 121; hereafter cited in text as "Heroic."
5. "George MacDonald: Nourishment for a Private World," *Reality and the Vision,* ed. Philip Yancy (Dallas: Word, 1990), 114; hereafter cited in text as *Nourishment*.
6. Jay Fox and James S. Jacobs, "An Interview with Madeleine L'Engle", *Literature and Belief* 7 (1987), 12; hereafter cited in the text.
7. *Summer of the Great-Grandmother* (1974; reprint, San Francisco: Harper and Row, 1980), 96–97; hereafter cited in the text as *Summer*.
8. *The Irrational Season* (1977; reprint, San Francisco: Harper and Row, 1980), 16; hereafter cited in the text as *Irrational*.
9. *A Circle of Quiet* (1972; reprint, San Francisco: Harper and Row, 1980), 19; hereafter cited in the text as *Circle*.
10. Sharon Donohue, "Unlikely Heroine," *Today's Christian Woman,* July/August 1990, 44; hereafter cited in the text.

11. *An Acceptable Time* (New York: Farrar, Straus and Giroux, 1989), 118; hereafter cited in the text as *Acceptable.*

12. "Is It Good Enough for Children," *The Writer,* April 1990, 13.

13. "Subject to Change Without Notice," *Theory into Practice* 21 (1982), 336.

14. "Fantasy Is What Fantasy Does," *Children's Literature in the Classroom: Weaving Charlotte's Web,"* eds. Janet Hickman and Bernice E. Cullinan (Needham Heights, Mass.: Christopher-Gordon, 1989), 130; hereafter cited in text as "Fantasy."

15. "Allegorical Fantasy: Mortal Dealings with Cosmic Questions," *Christianity Today,* 8 June 1979, 18; hereafter cited in text.

16. "Shake the Universe," *Ms.,* July/August 1987, 219.

17. Nathaniel Hawthorne, *Novels.* (Library of America. New York: Literary Classics of the United States, 1983).

18. "The One-Winged Chinese Bird," *Childhood Education* 50 (1974), 266; hereafter cited in text as "Bird."

19. Hugh Franklin, "Madeleine L'Engle," *Horn Book,* August 1963, 356.

20. *Dare to Be Creative* (Washington, D.C.: Library of Congress, 1984), 15; hereafter cited in text as *Dare.*

21. "The *Door* Interview," *Wittenburg Door,* January 1987, 23; hereafter cited in text as *Door.*

22. Ruth Moblard De Young, "Church Critics Battle L'Engle Heresy," *Banner,* 21 January 1991, 21.

23. John De Vries, "How the New Age Infiltrates," *Outlook,* November 1990, 11–13.

24. Joseph T. Vitale, "The Writer as Pray-er," *New Review of Books and Religion* 4 (1979), 4.

25. *A Stone for a Pillow: Journeys with Jacob* (Wheaton, Ill.: Harold Shaw, 1986), 87, 166; hereafter cited in text as *Stone.*

Chapter Two

1. *A Wrinkle in Time* (New York: Farrar, Straus and Giroux, 1962); hereafter cited in text as *Wrinkle.*

2. *A Wind in the Door* (New York: Farrar, Straus and Giroux, 1973); hereafter cited in text as *Wind.* Madeleine L'Engle, *A Swiftly Tilting Planet* (New York: Farrar, Straus and Giroux, 1978); hereafter cited in text as *Swiftly.*

3. Anne Devereaux Jordan, "Sugar 'n Spice 'n Snips 'n Snails: The Social-Sexual Role in Children's Fiction," *Sharing Literature with Chil-*

dren: A Thematic Anthology, ed. Francelia Butler (Prospect Heights, Ill.: Waveland, 1977), 347.

4. Janice Antczak, "The Growth and Development of a Genre," *Science Fiction: The Mythos of a New Romance* (New York: Neal-Schuman, 1985), 27.

5. Gary D. Schmidt, "See How They Grow: Character Development in Children's Series Books," *Children's Literature in Education* 18 (1989), 36; hereafter cited in text.

6. Jon Stott, "Midsummer Night's Dreams: Fantasy and Self-Realization in Children's Fiction," *The Lion and the Unicorn* 1 (1977), 25; hereafter cited in text.

7. Nancy Lou Patterson, "Angel and Psychopomp in Madeleine L'Engle's 'Wind' Trilogy," *Children's Literature in Education* 14 (1983), 195; hereafter cited in text.

8. "The Search for Truth," *Through the Eyes of a Child: An Introduction to Children's Literature,* ed. Donna E. Norton, 3rd ed. (New York: Macmillan, 1991), 325.

9. Sharon Gallagher, "Interview with Madeleine L'Engle," *Radix* 18 (1987), 12; hereafter cited in text.

10. Craig Wallace Barrow, "Recent Science Fiction and Science Fantasy," *Children's Literature* 5 (1976), 295.

11. William Blackburn, "Madeleine L'Engle's *A Wrinkle in Time:* Seeking the Original Face," *Touchstones: Reflections on the Best in Children's Literature,* vol. 1, ed. Perry Nodelman (West Lafayette, Ind.: Children's Literature Association, 1985), 125.

12. Carolyn Horowitz, "Only the Best," *Newbery and Caldecott Medal Books: 1956–65,* ed. Lee Kingman (Boston: Horn Book, 1965), 159.

13. "A Wrinkle in Time," Box Eight, Madeleine L'Engle Collection, de Grummond Children's Literature Research Collection, McCain Library and Archives, University of Southern Mississippi, Hattiesburg, Mississippi.

14. For an example of a less than favorable review, see Anita Silvey, "A Wind in the Door," *Horn Book* 49 (1973): 379. For examples of more favorable reviews see Jean Mercier, "A Wind in the Door," *Publisher's Weekly,* 16 April 1973, 54 or Michele Murray, "A Wind in the Door," *New York Times Book Review,* 8 July 1973, 8; hereafter cited in text.

15. *Intergalactic P.S.3* (New York: Children's Book Council, 1970); hereafter cited in text as *Intergalactic.*

16. Sarah Hayes, "Comic Cosmos," *Times Literary Supplement,* 4 April 1975, 360.

17. Wayne Dodd, "Mapping Numinous Ground," *Children's Literature* 4 (1975), 174.

18. Anne S. MacCleod, "Undercurrents: Pessimism in Contemporary Children's Literature," *Children's Literature in Education* 7 (1976), 101; hereafter cited in text.

19. *And It Was Good: Reflections on Beginnings* (Wheaton, Ill.: Shaw, 1983), 21; hereafter cited in text as *Good*.

20. "A Swiftly Tilting Planet," Box Twenty-eight, Published Manuscripts, Buswell Memorial Library Archives and Special Collections, Wheaton College, Wheaton, IL.

21. Barbara A. Bannon, "A Swiftly Tilting Planet," *Publisher's Weekly,* 3 July 1978, 65.

22. Review of *A Swiftly Tilting Planet, Kirkus Reviews* 46 (1978), 754.

23. Gary D. Schmidt, "The Story as Teller: An Interview with Madeleine L'Engle," *ALAN Review* 18 (1991), 14.

24. For a discussion of these types of charges, see Madeleine L'Engle, *Dare to Be Creative* (Washington: Library of Congress, 1984), 13–31.

Chapter Three

1. *The Twenty-four Days Before Christmas* (1984; reprint, New York, Dell, 1987); Madeleine L'Engle, *The Anti-Muffins* (New York: Pilgrim, 1980).

2. *Meet the Austins* (1960; reprint, New York: Dell, 1981) hereafter cited as *Austins;* Madeleine L'Engle, *The Moon by Night* (New York: Farrar, Straus and Giroux, 1963) hereafter cited as *Moon*; Madeleine L'Engle, *The Young Unicorns* (New York: Farrar, Straus and Giroux, 1968) hereafter cited as *Unicorns*; *A Ring of Endless Light* (New York: Farrar, Straus and Giroux, 1980) hereafter cited as *Ring*.

3. "The Triumph of the Human Spirit," in Butler, Francelia, and Rotert, Richard, eds., *Triumphs of the Spirit in Children's Literature* (Hamden: Library Professional Publications, 1986), xvi.

4. Review of *The Young Unicorns, Times Literary Supplement,* 16 October 1969, 529.

5. Geraldine E. La Rocgue, Review of *The Young Unicorns, English Journal* 58 (1969), 296; Review of *The Young Unicorns, New York Times Book Review,* 15 June 1980, 31.

6. Margaret P. Esmonde, "Beyond the Circles of the World: Death and the Hereafter in Children's Literature," *Webs and Wardrobes: Humanist and Religious World Views in Children's Literature,* eds. Joseph O'Beirne Milner and Lucy Floyd Morcock Milner (New York: University Press of America, 1987), 35.

7. Jane Abramson, "Facing the Other Fact of Life: Death in Recent Children's Fiction," *School Library Journal* 21 (1974), 33; hereafter cited in text.

8. Carol Van Strum, "Glimpses of the Grand Design," *Book World,* 11 May 1980, 15.

9. Jean Strouse, review of *A Ring of Endless Light, Newsweek,* 1 December 1980, 104; Marilyn Kaye, review of *A Ring of Endless Light, New York Times Book Review,* 11 January 1981, 29.

10. James W. Fowler, *Becoming Adult, Becoming Christian: Adult Development and Christian Faith* (San Francisco: Harper and Row, 1984), 60, 62.

11. Edmund Fuller, "Three Fine Stories of Life, Death and Enchantment," *Wall Street Journal,* 14 July 1980, 15.

12. "A Ring of Endless Light," Box Sixteen, Published Manuscripts, Buswell Memorial Library Archives and Special Collections, Wheaton College, Wheaton, Ill.

Chapter 4

1. "Before Babel," *Horn Book* 42 (1966), 666.

2. *A House like a Lotus* (New York: Farrar, Straus and Giroux, 1984); hereafter cited in text as *Lotus.* Madeleine L'Engle, *An Acceptable Time* (New York: Farrar, Straus and Giroux, 1989); hereafter cited in text as *Acceptable.* Madeleine L'Engle, *Dragons in the Waters* (New York: Farrar, Straus and Giroux, 1976); hereafter cited in text as *Dragons.* Madeleine L'Engle, *The Arm of the Starfish* (New York: Farrar, Straus and Giroux, 1965); hereafter cited in text as *Starfish.*

3. David Rees, *What Do Draculas Do? Essays on Contemporary Writers of Fiction for Children and Young Adults* (Metuchen, N.J.: Scarecrow, 1990), 60; hereafter cited in text. Rees is objecting here to Poly's language in *Dragons,* particularly one instance in which she paraphrases William Butler Yeats' "Second Coming" as she comments on the twentieth century to Simon.

4. "The Mysterious Appearance of Canon Tallis," *Spirit and Light: Essays in Historical Theology.* Edited by Madeleine L'Engle and William B. Green (New York: Seabury, 1976), 22.

5. Connie Soth, "'Listen to Your Work': An Interview with Madeleine L'Engle," *Arkenstone,* July/August 1980, 12; hereafter cited in text.

6. Sam L. Sebesta and William J. Iverson, *Literature for Thursday's Child* (Chicago: Science Research Associates, 1975), 234.

7. Ruth Hill Viguers, *Horn Book* 41 (April 1965), 161.

8. Cynthia Benjamin, *New York Times Book Review*, 20 June 1976, 22; hereafter cited in text.

9. "Books That Say Yes," *The Writer*, June 1976, 11; hereafter cited in text as "Books."

10. "Dragons in the Waters," Box Four, Published Manuscripts, Buswell Memorial Library Archives and Special Collections, Wheaton College, Wheaton, Ill.

11. "Acceptance Speech: Regina Medal Recipient," *Catholic Library World* 56 (July–August 1984), 31; hereafter cited in text as "Acceptance Speech."

12. Nancy E. Black, review of *A House like a Lotus, Voice of Youth Advocates*, April 1985, 50; Ethel R. Twichell, review of *A House like a Lotus, Horn Book* 61 (1985), 59; hereafter cited in text.

13. Roger D. Sutton, review of *A House like a Lotus, School Library Journal* 31 (December, 1984), 91; hereafter cited in text.

14. *An Acceptable Time* (New York: Farrar, Straus and Giroux, 1989), 37; hereafter cited in text as *Acceptable.*

15. For an example of this type of accusation, see Claris Van Kuiken, "Sojourning Into Darkness," *Christian Renewal*, 23 March 1992, 8.

16. Roger Sutton, review of *An Acceptable Time, Bulletin of the Center for Children's Books* 48:87. Christine Behrmann, review of *An Acceptable Time, School Library Journal* 36 (1990), 120. Sally Estes, review of *An Acceptable Time, Booklist*, 1 January 1990, 902; hereafter cited in text.

Chapter Five

1. *A Cry like a Bell* (Wheaton, Ill.: Shaw, 1987); Madeleine L'Engle, *The Journey with Jonah* (New York: Farrar, Straus and Giroux, 1967); Madeleine L'Engle, *Ladder of Angels* (New York: Seabury, 1979); Madeleine L'Engle, *The Glorious Impossible* (New York: Simon and Schuster, 1990).

2. *Many Waters* (New York: Farrar, Straus and Giroux, 1986); hereafter cited in text as *Waters;* Madeleine L'Engle, *Dance in the Desert* (New York: Farrar, Straus and Giroux, 1969) hereafter cited in text as *Desert*; Madeleine L'Engle, *The Sphinx at Dawn* (1982; San Francisco: Harper and Row, 1989); hereafter cited in text as *Sphinx.*

3. Christine Behrman, review of *Many Waters, School Library Journal*, 33 (1986), 104.

4. Susan Cooper, review of *Many Waters, New York Times Book Review*, 30 November 1986, 40.

5. Barbara A. Banmen, review of *Dance in the Desert, Publisher's Weekly,* 31 March 1969, 57.

6. Since this is an unpaginated text, I will refer to the narrative by noting the two-page spread on which it occurs, beginning with the first spread that contains text and illustration.

7. See, for example, *The Bestiary: A Book of Beasts.* edited by T. H. White, which says this about the unicorn: "He can be trapped by the following stratagem. A virgin girl is led to where he lurks, and there she is sent off by herself into the wood. He soon leaps into her lap when he sees her, and embraces her, and hence he gets caught (21).

8. *The Bestiary* explains the association of the pelican with Christ this way: "The Pelican is excessively devoted to its children. But when these have been born and begin to grow up, they flap their parents in the face with their wings, and their parents, striking back, kill them. Three days afterward the mother pierces her breast, opens her side, and lays herself across her young, pouring out her blood over the dead bodies. This brings them to life again.

In the same way, Our Lord Jesus Christ, who is the originator and maker of all created things, begets us and calls us into being out of nothing. We, on the contrary, strike him in the face. . . .

That was why he ascended into the height of the cross, and, his side having been pierced, there came from it blood and water for our salvation and eternal life" (133).

Chapter Six

1. *Camilla* (1951; reprint, New York: Delacorte, 1965); hereafter cited in text; Madeleine L'Engle, *And Both Were Young* (1949; reprint, New York: Dell, 1983); hereafter cited in text as *And Both;* Madeleine L'Engle, *The Small Rain* (1945; reprint, New York: Farrar, Straus and Giroux, 1984); hereafter cited in text as *Rain.*

2. Jan Cohn, *Romance and the Erotics of Property: Mass Market Fiction for Women* (Durham: Duke University Press, 1988), 18; hereafter cited in text.

3. John G. Cawelti, *Adventure, Mystery, and Romance: Formula Stories as Art and Popular Culture* (Chicago: University of Chicago Press, 1976), 270; hereafter cited in text.

4. Review of *And Both Were Young, Journal of Reading* 27, no. 4 (January 1984), 373.

5. Clare Boehmer, review of *And Both Were Young, Catholic Library World,* April 1984, 411.

6. Jean F. Mercier, review of *The Small Rain, Publisher's Weekly* 19 July 1985, 53.

7. Jennifer Crichton, "A Grab Bag of Great Reads," *Ms.,* June 1985, 68.

Afterword

1. John Rose Townsend. *A Sense of Story: Essays on Contemporary Writing for Children* (Philadelphia: Lippincott, 1971), 129.

2. M. Sarah Smedman, "Out of the Depths to Joy: Spirit/Soul in Juvenile Novels," in *Triumphs of the Spirit in Children's Literature*, eds. Francelia Butler and Richard Rotert (Hamden, Conn.: Library Professional Publications, 1986), 183.

Selected Bibliography

Primary Works

Novels

An Acceptable Time. New York: Farrar, Straus and Giroux, 1989.
And Both Were Young. 1949; New York: Dell, 1983.
The Anti-Muffins. New York: Pilgrim, 1980.
The Arm of the Starfish. New York: Farrar, Straus and Giroux, 1965.
Camilla. 1951; New York: Delacorte, 1965.
Dance in the Desert. New York: Farrar, Straus and Giroux, 1969.
Dragons in the Waters. New York: Farrar, Straus and Giroux, 1976.
A House like a Lotus. New York: Farrar, Straus and Giroux, 1984.
Ilsa. New York: Vanguard, 1946.
Many Waters. New York: Farrar, Straus and Giroux, 1986.
Meet the Austins. 1960; New York: Dell, 1981.
The Moon by Night. New York: Farrar, Straus and Giroux, 1963.
The Other Side of the Sun. New York: Farrar, Straus and Giroux, 1971.
A Ring of Endless Light. New York: Farrar, Straus and Giroux, 1980.
The Small Rain. 1945; New York: Farrar, Straus and Giroux, 1984.
The Sphinx at Dawn. San Francisco: Harper and Row, 1982.
A Swiftly Tilting Planet. New York: Farrar, Straus and Giroux, 1978.
The Twenty-four Days Before Christmas. 1984; New York: Dell, 1987.
A Wind in the Door. New York: Farrar, Straus and Giroux, 1973.
A Wrinkle in Time. New York: Farrar, Straus and Giroux, 1962.
The Young Unicorns. New York: Farrar, Straus and Giroux, 1968.

Nonfiction Books

And It Was Good: Reflections on Beginnings. Wheaton, Ill.: Shaw, 1983.
A Circle of Quiet. 1972. San Francisco: Harper and Row, 1980.

159

Dare to be Creative. Washington: Library of Congress, 1984.
The Irrational Season. 1977. San Francisco: Harper and Row, 1980.
Sold into Egypt: Joseph's Journey into Human Being. Wheaton, Ill.: Shaw, 1986.
A Stone for a Pillow: Journeys with Jacob. Wheaton, Ill.: Shaw, 1986.
The Summer of the Great-Grandmother. 1974. San Francisco: Harper and Row, 1980.
Trailing Clouds of Glory: Spiritual Values in Children's Literature. Edited by Madeleine L'Engle and Avery Brooke. Philadelphia: Westminster, 1985.
Two-Part Invention: The Story of a Marriage. New York: Farrar, Straus and Giroux, 1988.

Essays

"Acceptance Speech: Regina Medal Recipient." *Catholic Library World,* July/August 1984, 28–31.
"Angel Unaware." *The Other Side* November 1986, 34–37.
"Before Babel." *Horn Book* 42 (December 1966), 661–70.
"Books That Say Yes." *The Writer,* June 1976, 9–12.
"The Centipede and the Creative Spirit." *Horn Book* 45 August (1969): 373–77.
"Childlike Wonder and the Truths of Science Fiction." *Children's Literature* 10 (1982): 102–110.
"The Expanding Universe." *Horn Book* 39 (August 1963), 351–55.
"Fantasy Is What Fantasy Does." In *Children's Literature in the Classroom: Weaving Charlotte's Web,"* edited by Janet Hickman and Bernice E. Cullinan 129–33. Needham Heights, Mass.: Christopher-Gordon, 1989, 129–133.
"George McDonald: Nourishment for a Private World." In *Reality and the Vision: Eighteen Contemporary Writers Tell Who They Read and Why,* edited by Philip Yancy, 111–21. Dallas: Word, 1990.
"The Icon Tree." *Christian Century,* 6 April 1977, 321–24.
"In the Blood of the Lamb." *The Other Side,* June 1986, 24–27.
"Is It Good Enough for Children?" *The Writer,* April 1990, 11–13.
"The Key, the Door, the Road." *Horn Book,* 40 (June 1964), 260–68.
"The One-Winged Chinese Bird." *Childhood Education* 50 (1974), 266–73.
"Reflections on Faith and Art." *Other Side,* December 1982, 10–12.
"The Search for Truth." In *Through the Eyes of a Child: An Introduction to Children's Literature.* edited by Donna E. Norton. 3d ed., 324–25. New York: Macmillan, 1991.
"Shake the Universe." *Ms.,* July/August 1987, 182+.

"Sometimes I Forget to Tell You How Much I Love You." *Christianity Today,* 1 December 1978, 296–97.

"Subject to Change Without Notice." *Theory into Practice* 21 (1982), 332–38.

"Three Songs of Mary." *Horn Book* 39 (August 1963), 616–21.

"The Triumph of the Human Spirit." In *Triumphs of the Spirit in Children's Literature,* edited by Francelia Butler and Richard Rotert, XV–XVII. Hamden, Conn.: Library Professional Publications, 1986.

"We of the Broken Body." *Commonweal,* 26 May 1978, 331–33.

"What Is Real?" *Language Arts,* April 1978, 447–51.

Secondary Works

Interviews

Braver, Barbara Leix. "Becoming More Human: An Interview with Madeleine L'Engle." *Christian Century,* 20 November 1985, 1067–1068.

Cully, Kendig Brubaker. "An Interview With Madeleine L'Engle." *Review of Books and Religion* (October 1981), 6–7.

Donahue, Sharon. "Unlikely Heroine." *Today's Christian Woman,* July/August 1990, 43–45.

Forbes, Cheryl. "Allegorical Fantasy: Mortal Dealings with Cosmic Questions." *Christianity Today* 8 June 1979, 4–19.

Gallagher, Sharon. "Interview with Madeleine L'Engle." *Radix* 18, no. 3 (1987): 12–15.

Jacobs, James S., and Jay Fox. "An Interview with Madeleine L'Engle." *Literature and Belief* 7 (1987): 1–16.

"Madeleine L'Engle: The Door Interview." *Wittenburg Door,* December 1986/January 1987, 23–29.

Schmidt, Gary D. "The Story as Teller: An Interview with Madeleine L'Engle." *ALAN Review* 18, no. 2 (1991), 10–14.

Soth, Connie. "'Listen to Your Work': An Interview with Madeleine L'Engle." *Arkenstone,* July/August 1980, 9–17.

Vitale, Joseph T. "The Writer as Pray-er: An Interview with Madeleine L'Engle." *New Review of Books and Religion* 4 (November 1979), 4.

Articles and Books

Abramson, Jane. "Facing the Other Fact of Life: Death in Recent Children's Fiction." *School Library Journal* 21 (1974): 31–33.

162   *Selected Bibliography*

Adams, Karen I. "Madeleine L'Engle: Writing as an Incarnational Vocation." *Literature and Belief* 7 (1987): 17–25.
Antczak, Janice. "The Growth and Development of a Genre." In *Science Fiction: The Mythos of a New Romance,* edited by Jane Anne Hannigan. New York: Neal-Schuman, 1985, 15–37.
Barrow, Craig Wallace. "Recent Sience Fiction and Science Fantasy," *Children's Literature* 5 (1976): 294–297.
Blackburn, William. "Madeleine L'Engle's *A Wrinkle in Time:* Seeking the Original Face." In *Touchstones: Reflections on the Best in Children's Literature.* Vol. 1., edited by Perry Nodelman, 123–131. West Lafayette, Ind.: Children's Literature Association, 1985.
Boice, Linda. "Have the Dragons All Been Vanquished?" *Eternity,* July/August 1985, 17–23.
Brett, Sally. "Four Approaches to the Truth About Christmas." *Books & Religion,* December 1986, 6–8.
Carlson, G. Robert. "Forty Years with Books and Teen-Age Readers." In *Young Adult Literature in the Seventies: A Selection of Readings,* edited by Jana Varlejs, 70–76. Metuchen, N.J.: Scarecrow, 1978.
Cawelti, John G. *Adventure, Mystery, and Romance: Formula Stories as Art and Popular Culture.* Chicago: University of Chicago Press, 1976.
Cohn, Jan. *Romance and the Erotics of Property: Mass Market Fiction for Women.* Durham: Duke University Press, 1988.
Cully, Kendig Brubaker. "An Interview with Madeleine L'Engle." *Review of Books and Religion* (October 1981), 6–7.
De Vries, John. "How the New Age Infiltrates." *Outlook,* November 1990, 11–13.
De Young, Ruth Moblard. "Church Critics Battle L'Engle 'Heresy.'" *The Banner,* 21 January 1991, pp. 21–22.
Dodd, Wayne. "Mapping Numinous Ground." *Children's Literature* 4 (1975): 173–75.
Esmonde, Margaret P. "Beyond the Circles of the World: Death and the Hereafter in Children's Literature." In *Webs and Wardrobes: Humanist and Religious World Views in Children's Literature,* edited by Joseph O'Beirne Milner and Lucy Floyd Morcock Milner, 34–45. New York: University Press of America, 1987.
Forbes, Cheryl. "Supernatural Sagas of Good and Evil: The Foolish Things of Madeleine L'Engle." *Christianity Today,* 8 June 1979, 30–31.
Fowler, James W. *Becoming Adult, Becoming Christian: Adult Development and Christian Faith.* San Francisco: Harper and Row, 1984.
Franklin, Hugh. "Madeleine L'Engle." *Horn Book* 39 (August 1963), 356–60.

Hampton, Barbara J. "Sense and Censorship." *Eternity,* September 1983, 18–24.

Horowitz, Carolyn. "Only the Best." *Newbery and Caldecott Medal Books: 1956–65,* edited by Lee Kingman, 153–62. Boston: Horn Book, 1965.

Jordan, Anne Devereaux. "Sugar 'n Spice 'n Snips 'n Snails: The Social-Sexual Role in Children's Fiction." In *Sharing Literature with Children: A Thematic Anthology,* edited by Francelia Butler. Prospect Heights, Ill.: Waveland, 1977.

Kehl, D. G. "Clerics and the Elderly in the Contemporary Novel." *Journal of Religion & Aging* 4 (1987), 1–20.

Lagerwey, Mary Boerman. "A Passion for What's Real." *The Banner,* 1 October 1990, 12–13.

Lefever, Marlene. "Beyond the Divorce of Faith and Art." *Christianity Today,* 22 February 1980, 82–83.

Lorentzen, Mel. "Madeline L'Engle: Making Us Feel More Human." *The Other Side,* November 1986, 42–44.

Lynch, Margaret Bach. "L'Engle and the Year of the Child." *New Review of Books and Religion* 4 (November 1979), 5.

Mac Cleod, Anne S. "Undercurrents: Pessimism in Contemporary Children's Literature." *Children's Literature in Education* 7 (Summer 1976), 96–102.

Morgan, Argiro L. "Reading Between the Lines of Dialogue in Children's Books: Using the Pragmatics of Language." *Children's Literature in Education* 20 (December 1989), 227–37.

Patterson, Nancy Lou. "Angel and Psychopomp in Madeleine L'Engle's 'Wind' Trilogy." *Children's Literature in Education* 14 (Winter 1983), 195–203.

Rosenfeld, Judith B. "Books in the Classroom." *Horn Book* 64 (January/February 1988), 105–106.

Schmidt, Gary D. "See How They Grow: Character Development in Children's Series Books." *Children's Literature in Education* 18 (Spring 1987), 34–44.

Sebesta, Sam L. and William J. Iverson. *Literature for Thursday's Child.* Chicago: Science Research Associates, 1975.

Smedman, M. Sarah. "Out of the Depths to Joy: Spirit/Soul in Juvenile Novels." In *Triumphs of the Spirit in Children's Literature,* edited by Francelia Butler and Richard Rotert, 181–197. Hamden, Conn.: Library Professional Publications, 1986.

Stott, Jon. "Midsummer Night's Dreams: Fantasy and Self-Realization in Children's Fiction." *The Lion and the Unicorn* 1, no. 2 (Fall 1977), 25–39.

Van Atta, Lucibel. "This Is No Time to Have a Baby . . . Or Is It?" *Moody,* May 1980, 33–34.

Vaughan, Henry. *Henry Vaughan: The Complete Poems,* edited by Alan Rudrum. New Haven: Yale University Press, 1981.

Wimbish, David. "Wind of the Spirit Blows into Some Secular Bookstores." *Charisma,* May 1983, 84.

Wolf, Virginia L. "Readers of *Alice:* My Children, Meg Murry, and Harriet M. Welsch." *Children's Literature Association Quarterly* 13 (1988), 135–37.

Selected Book Reviews

A House like a Lotus
Black, Nancy E. *Voice of Youth Advocates* 8 (April 1985), 50.
Mercier, Jean F. *Publisher's Weekly* 2 November 1984, 77.
Sutton, Roger D. *School Library Journal* 31 (December 1984), 91.
Twichell, Ethel R. *Horn Book* 61 (January/February 1985), 59.

An Acceptable Time
Behrmann, Christine. *School Library Journal* 36 (January 1990), 120.
Estes, Sally. *Booklist,* 1 January 1990, 902.
Sutton, Roger. *Bulletin of the Center for Children's Books* 48, no. 1 (1989), 87.

And Both Were Young
English Journal 72 (October 1983), 86.
Journal of Reading 27, no. 4 (1984), 373.
Zvirvin, Stephanie. *Booklist,* 1 March 1983, 870+.

A Swiftly Tilting Planet
Bannon, Barbara A. *Publisher's Weekly,* 3 July 1978, 65.
Booklist, 1 July 1978, 1679.
Kirkus Reviews 46 (1978), 754.
Norsworthy, James. *Catholic Library World,* 50 April 1979, 402–403.
Prescott, Peter S. *Newsweek,* 18 December 1978, 102.
Williams, Paul O. "L'Engle Travels Through Time." *Christian Science Monitor,* 23 October 1978, sec. B, 8.
"The Empty Houses in Tinsel Town." *The Economist,* 27 December 1980, 73–76.

A Wind in the Door
Mercier, Jean. "A Wind in the Door," *Publisher's Weekly* 16 April 1973, 54.

Murray, Michele. "A Wind in the Door," *New York Times Book Review,* 8 July 1973, 8.
Silvey, Anita. *Horn Book* 49, August 1973, 379–380.

A Wrinkle in Time
Beard, P.D. *Library Journal* 15 March 1962, 1332.
Buell, E.L. *New York Times Book Review,* 18 March 1962, 29.
Saturday Review, 12 May 1962, 40.
Viguers, Ruth Hill. *Horn Book* 38 (April 1962), 177.

Camilla
Elleman, Barbara. *Booklist,* 1 November 1981, 378, 390.
Gerhardt, Lillian. *School Library Journal* 28 (March 1982), 160.

Dance in the Desert
Banmen, Barbara A. *Publisher's Weekly,* 31 March 1969, 57.
Cullen, Elinor. *Library Journal,* July 1969, 2672.
Stoltz, Mary. *New York Times Book Review,* 10 August 1969, 20.
Viguers, Ruth Hill. *Horn Book* 45 (August 1969), 400–401.

Dragons in the Waters
Benjamin, Cynthia. *New York Times Book Review,* 20 June 1976, 22.
Kennerly, S.L. *School Library Journal* 23 (March 1976), 78.
Robinson, Beryl. *Horn Book,* 52 (August 1976), 405–406.
Weir, Emily. *Best Sellers,* August 1976, 151.

Many Waters
Behrman, Christine. *School Library Journal* 33 (November 1986), 104.
Cooper, Susan. *New York Times Book Review,* 30 November 1986, 40.
Murphy, Susie. *Journal of Reading* 32, no. 1 (1988), 89.
Stuttaford, Genevieve. *Publisher's Weekly,* 31 October 1986, 70+.

The Arm of the Starfish
Dagliesh, Alice. *Saturday Review,* 24 April 1965, 45.
Hood, Robert. *New York Times Book Review,* 18 April 1965, 16.
Light, Carolyn M. *Best Sellers,* 15 April 1965, 36.
Maxwell, Emily. *New Yorker,* 4 December 1965, 244.
Viguers, Ruth Hill. *Horn Book* 41 (April 1965), 161.

The Small Rain
Mercier, Jean F. *Publisher's Weekly,* 19 July 1985, 53.
Crichton, Jennifer. "A Grab Bag of Great Reads," *Ms,* June 1985, 68.

Index

167

The Author

Donald R. Hettinga is Professor of English at Calvin College where he teaches courses in children's literature and writing. Among his other books are *Sitting at the Feet of the Past: Retelling the North American Folktale for Children* and *In the World: Reading and Writing for Christians*. A graduate of The University of Chicago, where he was a Whiting Fellow, Hettinga now lives in Grand Rapids, Michigan, with his wife, Kimberly, and their four children—Caitlin, Ariel, Zane, and Dylan.

The Editor

Patricia J. (Patty) Campbell is an author and critic specializing in books for young adults. She has taught adolescent literature at University of California–Los Angeles and is the former assistant coordinator of Young Adult Services for Los Angeles Public Library. Her literary criticism has been published in the *New York Times Book Review* and many other journals. From 1978 to 1988 her column, "The YA Perplex," a monthly review of young adult books, appeared in the *Wilson Library Bulletin*. She now writes a review column on the independent press for that magazine. Campbell is the author of five books, among them *Presenting Robert Cormier,* the first volume in the Twayne Young Adult Author Series. In 1989 she was the recipient of the American Library Association Grolier Award for distinguished achievement with young people and books. A native of Los Angeles, Campbell presently lives on an avocado ranch near San Diego, where she and her husband David Shore write and publish books on overseas camper van travel.